Revised Edition

Instant Japanese
Phrase Book

**How to express 1000 different ideas
with just 100 key words and phrases**

by Boye De Mente
revised by Henk de Groot & Yasuko Tsuji

D0424381

TUTTLE PUBLISHING
Boston • Rutland, Vermont • Tokyo

Published by Tuttle Publishing, an imprint of Periplus Editions
with editorial offices at 153 Milk Street, Boston, MA 02109 and
130 Joo Seng Road #06-01/03, Singapore 368357

Copyright © 1993 by Charles E. Tuttle Publishing Co., Inc.
Copyright © 2003 Periplus Editions (HK) Ltd.

LCC Card Number: 93-60054
ISBN 0-8048-3366-4

Printed in Canada

Distributed by:

Japan
Tuttle Publishing
Yaekari Building 3F
5-4-12 Osaki, Shinagawa-ku
Tokyo 141-0032, Japan
Tel: (03) 5437 0171   Fax: (03) 5437 0755
Email: tuttle-sales@gol.com

North America, Latin America & Europe
Tuttle Publishing
364 Innovation Drive
North Clarendon, VT 05759-9436, USA
Tel: (802) 773 8930   Fax: (802) 773 6993
Email: info@tuttlepublishing.com
www.tuttlepublishing.com

Asia Pacific
Berkeley Books Pte Ltd
130 Joo Seng Road, 06-01/03
Singapore 368357
Tel: (65) 6280 1330   Fax: (65) 6280 6290
Email: inquiries@periplus.com.sg
www.periplus.com

08 07 06 05
8 7 6 5 4 3

Contents

Preface

A little language goes a long way!

It is a well-established fact that most people of average intelligence and education use a vocabulary of only five or six hundred words in going about their daily lives. The reason for this is that it is possible to express a variety of thoughts by using various forms of a single word. Each additional word exponentially increases the number of thoughts one can express. Another obvious reason why a limited vocabulary is enough to get most people through a day is because they are primarily involved in basic situations that are repeated day after day.

The Japanese language is especially flexible because there are so many "set" expressions found in common, everyday situations. One can, for example, express over ten complete thoughts by using the different forms of a single Japanese verb. Mastering just ten verbs and their forms therefore makes it possible to say over one hundred things.

This handy guide is designed to show how a very small vocabulary is enough to quickly and fluently communicate over 1,000 ideas in Japanese. And because Japanese can be easily rendered into English phonetics, virtually all problems with pronunciation can be eliminated.

Instant Japanese contains a phoneticized pronunciation guide and all the key words and expressions you need to cover most of the personal situations you are likely to encounter during a visit to Japan.

Writing Japanese

There are four different ways of writing the Japanese language —although one of them is generally limited to foreign words written phonetically so they can be pronounced easily. These four ways are:

1. **Kanji** （かんじ） or logograms (originally imported from China), which are used together with a phonetic script called *hiragana* （ひらがな）。 This is the standard and most common way of writing Japanese.

2. **Hiragana** （ひらがな） is a phonetic script that is used (together with **kanji**) for verb endings, prepositions, etc. In texts written for children it is common to use only **hiragana**, because that is what they first learn to read.

3. **Katakana** （カタカナ） This is another phonetic script, and is primarily reserved for transcribing foreign words into Japanese syllables. For example, the Japanese word for "hotel" is *hoteru* （ホテル）, and is always written in **katakana** script.

　　With the exception of the vowels **a**, **i**, **u**, **e** and **o** and the consonant **n**, all **hiragana** and **katakana** consist of a consonant-vowel combination.

4. **Rōmaji** （ローマじ）, or "Roman letters," was originally used by and for the benefit of foreigners who could not read **kanji** or **hiragana**. It is now commonly used on signs all over Japan—usually in conjunction with **kanji**, **hiragana**, or both. The reading and writing of Romanized Japanese (**Rōmaji**) is not taught as a regular course in public schools,

so only those who study privately develop skill in reading it. **Rōmaji** is, however, commonly used on a variety of school materials, advertising, shop signs and so on, though sometimes, it seems, just for exotic effect.

In this book, all Japanese words and expressions are presented in **Rōmaji** as well as in **hiragana** or **katakana**. For correct pronunciation, refer to the explanations and the chart on the following pages.

How to Pronounce Japanese

The Japanese language is very easy to pronounce. It is made up of precise syllables that are based on just five vowel sounds: **a** (as in "**ah**"), **i** (as in "fr**ee**"), **u** (as in "b**oo**"), **e** (as in "m**et**"), and **o** (as in "s**o**", only shorter).

When consonant sounds are added to these vowel sounds, syllables are created which follow the same sound pattern: **ka** (か), **ki** (き), **ku** (く), **ke** (け), **ko** (こ), and **sa** (さ), **shi** (し), **su** (す), **se** (せ), **so** (そ), and so forth.

In Japanese, the **H** and **G** sounds are always pronounced as in "how" and "go." There are no true **L** or **V** sounds in Japanese; thus they do not appear in the list of syllables. When the Japanese attempt to pronounce these sounds in English words, the **L** comes out as **R** and the **V** comes out as **B**.

All you have to do to pronounce these syllables (and the words they make up) correctly, is to voice them according to the phonetics taught in this book. When you pronounce the Japanese words and phrases phonetically, the sounds come out "in Japanese."

あ E-し, い), U-ーラ e-ー1え O-ー1あ-お
フカ, か K-ーニキ,き, ku-く ke-1,い-け, ko-こ
ー1さ, shi-し, su-し, す, se-ー1せ, せ so-そ

Kana and Pronunciation Chart

This chart contains all of the syllables that make up the sounds in the Japanese language, along with their **hiragana** and **katakana** equivalents.

A	I	U	E	O
あ(ア)	い(イ)	う(ウ)	え(エ)	お(オ)
KA	**KI**	**KU**	**KE**	**KO**
か(カ)	き(キ)	く(ク)	け(ケ)	こ(コ)
SA	**SHI**	**SU**	**SE**	**SO**
さ(サ)	し(シ)	す(ス)	せ(セ)	そ(ソ)
	looks like piece of hair		looks like seaman	looks like PicaSO
TA	**CHI**	**TSU**	**TE**	**TO**
た(タ)	ち(チ)	つ(ツ)	て(テ)	と(ト)
looks like TA	looks like CHEAP 5		TErrible	looks like a Toe
NA	**NI**	**NU**	**NE**	**NO**
な(ナ)	に(二)	ぬ(ヌ)	ね(ネ)	の(ノ)
	Nine is before 10	looks like Noodles		NO sign
HA	**HI**	**FU**	**HE**	**HO**
は(ハ)	ひ(ヒ)	ふ(フ)	へ(ヘ)	ほ(ホ)
		looks like 'a nose		High mountain
MA	**MI**	**MU**	**ME**	**MO**
ま(マ)	み(ミ)	む(ム)	め(メ)	も(モ)
YA		**YU**		**YO**
や(ヤ)		ゆ(ユ)		よ(ヨ)
RA	**RI**	**RU**	**RE**	**RO**
ら(ラ)	り(リ)	る(ル)	れ(レ)	ろ(ロ)
WA				**(W)O**
わ(ワ)				を

(margin handwritten notes: "looks like", "other sounds", "these are lower sounds", "family sounds")

How to Pronounce Japanese Words   7

GA	**GI**	**GU**	**GE**	**GO**
が（ガ）	ぎ（ギ）	ぐ（グ）	げ（ゲ）	ご（ゴ）

ZA	**JI**	**ZU**	**ZE**	**ZO**
ざ（ザ）	じ（ジ）	ず（ズ）	ぜ（ゼ）	ぞ（ゾ）

DA	**JI**	**ZU**	**DE**	**DO**
だ（ダ）	ぢ（ヂ）	づ（ヅ）	で（デ）	ど（ド）

BA	**BI**	**BU**	**BE**	**BO**
ば（バ）	び（ビ）	ぶ（ブ）	べ（ベ）	ぼ（ボ）

PA	**PI**	**PU**	**PE**	**PO**
ぱ（パ）	ぴ（ピ）	ぷ（プ）	ぺ（ペ）	ぽ（ポ）

The **R** sound in Japanese is close to the **L** sound in English, requiring a slight trilling sound to get it right. It resembles the **R** sound in Spanish.

The following syllables are combinations of some of those appearing above. The two primary syllables are combined into one simply by merging the pronunciations. Pronounce the **Y** here as you do in the word "yes."

KYA	**KYU**	**KYO**
きゃ（キャ）	きゅ（キュ）	きょ（キョ）

SHA	**SHU**	**SHO**
しゃ（シャ）	しゅ（シュ）	しょ（ショ）

CHA	**CHU**	**CHO**
ちゃ（チャ）	ちゅ（チュ）	ちょ（チョ）

NYA	**NYU**	**NYO**
にゃ（ニャ）	にゅ（ニュ）	にょ（ニョ）

HYA	**HYU**	**HYO**
ひゃ(ヒャ)	ひゅ(ヒュ)	ひょ(ヒョ)

MYA	**MYU**	**MYO**
みゃ(ミャ)	み(ミュ)	みょ(ミョ)

RYA	**RYU**	**RYO**
りゃ(リャ)	りゅ(リュ)	りょ(リョ)
		(Roll the *R* a bit)

GYA	**GYU**	**GYO**
ぎゃ(ギャ)	ぎゅ(ギュ)	ぎょ(ギョ)

JA	**JU**	**JO**
じゃ(ジャ)	じゅ(ジュ)	じょ(ジョ)

BYA	**BYU**	**BYO**
びゃ(ビャ)	びゅ(ビュ)	びょ(ビョ)

PYA	**PYU**	**PYO**
ぴゃ(ピャ)	ぴゅ(ピュ)	ぴょ(ピョ)

N
ん(ン)

Keep in mind that the sounds in the chart above are to be pronounced as one syllable, not two. Native English speakers often find **rya** りゃ, **ryu** りゅ, and **ryo** りょ the hardest to pronounce as one syllable. Try asking a native speaker to say them for you so you can hear how they should sound.

There are long, short, and silent vowels in Japanese, as well as double consonants. Long vowels are shown in **Rōmaji** (that is, the Western alphabet) by a macron (a little mark above the letter ā means a doubled **aa** sound). In **hira-**

gana, they are represented by a following vowel (for **a** that is always an extra **i**, for **e** and **i** another **i**, and for the others usually an **u**), while in **katakana** the sound is simply extended by a small bar: ─.

Examples:

sābisu	サービス	(service)
oishii	おいしい	(delicious)
kūkō	くうこう	(airport)
eiga	えいが	(movie)

To get the most out of this guide, first practice pronouncing the syllables—out loud—until you can enunciate each one easily without having to think about it. Before long you will be able to recognize individual syllables in the Japanese words you hear.

Then go to the key-word and key-phrase portion of the book and practice pronouncing each word and sentence, repeating the words and sentences aloud until you can get them out in a smooth flow.

You'll be happy to find that you can communicate in Japanese instantly—simply by following the pronunciation instructions consistently.

PART 1
Words 1–10

1 ohayō gozaimasu *(oh-hai-yoe go-zai-mahss)*
good morning おはよう　ございます

Unlike the English "Good morning", which can be used right up until lunchtime, **ohayō gozaimasu** is normally only said when you meet someone first thing in the morning, up until about 11 a.m..

2 konnichi wa *(kone-nee-chee wah)*
good afternoon こんにち　は

Note that the **wa** *(wah)* は, when it stands alone, is pronounced **wa**. See p. 16 for an explanation of the grammatical particle **wa**.

3 konban wa *(kome-bahn wah)*
good evening こんばん　は

4 dōmo arigatō *(doe-moe ah-ree-gah-toe)*
thank you very much どうも　ありがとう

5 sumimasen *(sue-me-mah-sen)*
pardon me, excuse me, I am sorry, thank you.
すみません

Because of its variety of meanings, **sumimasen** is an extremely useful word. Use it liberally. It is often shortened to **simasen.**

6 dōzo *(doe-zoe)*
please どうぞ

This is one of the many words that means "please" in Japanese. **Dōzo** is used in the sense of "please go first," "please continue," or "after you."

7 kudasai *(koo-dah-sai)*
please ください

This word for "please give me" is almost never used by itself. Rather, it normally follows the command form of verbs as in **tabete kudasai** *(tah-bay-tay koo-dah-sai)* たべて ください, "please eat," or **nonde kudasai** *(noan-day koo-dah-sai)* のんで ください, "please drink." It is also used with nouns to convey the meaning of "please," as in "please bring me water" or "please hand me that."

8 mizu *(me-zoo)*
water みず

➡ Please give me (a glass of) water. みず を ください
Mizu o kudasai. *(me-zoo oh koo-dah-sai)*

O *(oh)* を is a grammatical particle used to indicate that the preceding word is the direct object of the action—in this example, water. There are no indefinite or definite articles (a, the) in Japanese, and only a few plural forms.

9 watashi *(wah-tah-she)*
I わたし

There are several commonly used terms in Japanese for the word "I," based on gender and other factors, but **watashi** *(wah-tah-she)* わたし is common and can be used by anyone in any situation.

10 watakushi *(wah-tock-she)*
I (formal) わたくし

Watakushi can be used by both men and women in formal as well as informal situations.

Developing Verbal Skill

In order to develop verbal fluency in Japanese, it is necessary to train the mouth as well as the mind. Simply memorizing words and sentences on a page is obviously not enough. You must be able to say the words or sentences clearly enough that they can be understood.

This means that you must physically train your mouth and tongue to say the foreign words properly—to get them out in a smooth, even flow. In other words, language learning (if you wish to speak the language) must be approached as a physical skill, like juggling, playing the guitar, or singing.

For example, pronunciation of the Japanese word **dō itashimashite** *(doe-ee-tah-she-mahssh-tay)* どう いたしまして or "don't mention it," requires seven different tongue and mouth positions. The only way you can master this phrase is to say it over and over again, preferably out loud, because this increases confidence in your ability to say it and trains your hearing at the same time.

The key to learning how to speak Japanese is to speak it repeatedly—not just read it or read about it—until it comes out automatically, without you having to work too hard. Repeating words and sentences out loud, **kurikaeshi kurikaeshi** *(koo-ree-kai-eh-she koo-ree-kai-eh-she)* くりかえ し くりかえし—"over and over again"—is the key to developing verbal skill in any language.

PART 2
Words 11–20

11 watashi ni *(wah-tah-she nee)*
to me わたしに

Ni *(nee)* に is a grammatical particle that can indicate
that the preceding word is the indirect object of the
action. In this instance **ni** changes "I" to "me" as in "to
me" or "for me."

12 watashi no *(wah-tah-she no)*
my, mine わたしの

No *(no)* の is a grammatical particle that can change
what precedes it to the possessive case. In this example,
adding **no** to **watashi** changes "I" to "my" or "mine."

13 watashi-tachi / watashi-tachi no
(wah-tah-she-tah-chee / wah-tah-she-tah-chee no)
we / our, ours わたしたち／わたしたち　の

Adding **-tachi** *(-tah-chee)* たち to personal pronouns
("I," "you," "she" etc.) makes them plural.

14 desu *(dess)*
am, is, are です

Desu *(dess)* です is a polite word without meaning, but
can be thought of as functioning like the verb "to be" in
English. Neither **desu** nor any of its forms (see following page) are used by themselves, but they are as essen-
tial for making correct, complete sentences in Japanese
as the English "I am," "you are," "he is," and so forth.
The plain form of **desu** is **da** *(dah)* だ.

15 de wa arimasen *(day wah ah-ree-mah-sen)*
am not, is not, are not で は ありません

Plain forms of this include **de wa nai** *(day wah nai)* で
は ない and **ja nai** *(jah nai)* じゃ ない.

16 deshita *(desh-tah)*
was, were でした

The plain form of this is **datta** *(dah-tah)* だった.

17 de wa arimasen deshita
(day wah ah-ree-mah-sen desh-tah)
was not, were not. で は ありません でした

Plain forms of this include **de wa nakatta** *(day wah
nah-kaht-tah)* で は なかった and **ja nakatta** *(jah
nah-kaht-tah)* じゃ なかった.

18 namae *(nah-my)*
name なまえ

➡ My name is Boyé De Mente.
わたし の なまえ は ボイデメンテ です。
Watashi no namae wa Boyé De Mente desu.
(wah-tah-she no nah-my wah Boye De Mente dess)

Wa *(wah)* は is a grammatical particle used to indicate
that the preceding word or words are the topic in a sentence.

➡ My name is not Smith.
わたし の なまえ は スミス で は ありません。
Watashi no namae wa Sumisu de wa arimasen.
*(wah-tah-she no nah-my wah sue-me-sue day wah ah-
ree-mah-sen)*

17 nan / nani *(nahn / nahn-nee)*
what なん／なに

18 anata / anata no *(ah-nah-tah / ah-nah-tah no)*
you / your, yours あなた／あなた の

The word **anata** *(ah-nah-tah)* あなた is normally best avoided, since it can convey inappropriate familiarity. Where possible, address people by their name, or drop the word for "you" entirely (see examples 20 and 21). Another option is for you to use the honorific prefix **O-**. For example:

➡ What is your name? おなまえ は なん です か。
O-namae wa nan desu ka?* *(oh nah-my wah nahn dess kah)*

Ka *(kah)* か at the end of a sentence makes it a question.

19 Amerika-jin *(ah-may-ree-kah-jeen)*
an American person or American people アメリカじん

➡ I am American.
わたし は アメリカじん です。
Watashi wa Amerika-jin desu.
(wah-tah-she wah ah-may-ree-kah-jeen dess)

20 Nihon-jin *(nee-hone-jeen)*
a Japanese person or people にほんじん

➡ Are you Japanese?
にほんじん です か。
Nihon-jin desu ka?
(nee-hone-jeen dess kah)

➡ We are British.
わたしたち は イギリスじん です。
Watashi-tachi wa Igirisu-jin desu.
(wah-tah-she-tah-chee wah ee-gee-ree-soo-jeen dess)

➡ I am Canadian. わたし は カナダじん です。
Watashi wa Kanada-jin desu.
(wah-tah-she wah kah-nah-dah-jeen dess)

➡ We are Australian.
わたしたち は オーストラリアじん です。
Watashi-tachi wa Øsutoraria-jin desu.
(wah-tah-she-tah-chee oh-sue-toe-rah-ree-ah-jeen dess)

Double Consonants

Many words in Japanese have double consonants that beginning speakers mispronounce. This can result in language that sounds like gibberish or something entirely different from what is intended. There is an easy way to overcome this problem because Japanese is a language made up of precise syllables. The double consonant is represented in hiragana by a smaller-sized **tsu** *(t'sue)* つ, which is not pronounced, but which occupies a period of time (a "beat") equivalent to that of the other **hiragana**.

All you have to do is mentally divide the sounds of such words into their phonetic equivalents (as all Japanese words are in this book), and account for the double consonant sounds by allowing for an extra "beat" for the small **tsu**. Try pronouncing the following examples. To pronounce these words correctly, just say each of the individual phonetic syllables fully and clearly. You will hear a very slight pause before the double consonants, similar to the sound in the English word "bookkeeper."

kekkō *(keck-ko)*
fine, alright けっこう

matte kudasai *(maht-tay koo-dah-sai)*
please wait まって　ください

itte kudasai *(eet-tay koo-dah-sai)*
please go いって　ください

tomatte kudasai *(toe-maht-tay koo-dah-sai)*
please stop とまって　ください

haitte kudasai *(hite-tay koo-dah-sai)*
please come in はいって　ください

gakkō *(gahk-ko)*
school がっこう

yukkuri *(yuke-koo-ree)*
slow ゆっくり

PART 3
Words 21–30

21 donata / donata no *(doe-nah-tah / doe-nah-tah no)*
who / whose どなた ／どなた　の

Who are you? どなた　です　か。
Donata desu ka? *(doe-nah-tah dess kah)*

22 kore *(koe-ray)*
this これ

➡ Whose is this? これ　は　どなた　の　です　か。
Kore wa donata no desu ka?
(koe-ray wah doe-nah-tah no dess kah)

➡ It is mine. わたし　の　です。
Watashi no desu. *(wah-tah-she no dess)*
(The "it" is understood)

➡ It is ours. わたしたち　の　です。
Watashi-tachi no desu. *(wah-tah-she-tah-chee no dess)*

23 sore *(soe-ray)*
that それ

➡ What is that? それ　は　なん　です　か。
Sore wa nan desu ka? *(soe-ray wah nahn dess kah)*

➡ Whose is that? それ　は　どなた　の　です　か。
Sore wa donata no desu ka?
(soe-ray wah doe-nah-tah no dess kah)

➡ Is that yours? それ は …さん の です か。
Sore wa (person's name)-san no desu ka?
(soe-ray wah …-san no dess kah)

24 ano hito / ano hito no
(ah-no-ssh-toe / ah-no-ssh-toe no)
he, she, him, her / his, hers あの ひと／あの ひと の

➡ That is hers. それ は あの ひと の です。
Sore wa ano hito no desu.
(soe-ray wah ah-no-ssh-toe no dess)

➡ Who is that? あの ひと は どなた です か。
Ano hito wa donata desu ka?
(ah-no-ssh-toe wah doe-nah-tah dess kah)

➡ What is his name?
あの ひと の なまえ は なん です か。
Ano hito no namae wa nan desu ka?
(ah-no-ssh-toe no nah-my wah nahn dess kah)

➡ His name is Green. グリーン です。
Gurīn desu. *(goo-reen dess)*
("his name" is understood)

25 messēji *(may-say-jee)*
message メッセージ

➡ Do you have a message for me?
わたし に メッセージ が ありますか。
Watashi ni messēji ga arimasu ka?
(wah-tah-she nee may-say-jee gah ah-ree-mahss kah)

Ga *(gah)* が is similar to **wa** *(wah)* は, but normally indicates the grammatical subject of a sentence or phrase. Once a subject or topic has been mentioned at the beginning of a conversation, it is often deleted from subsequent sentences, which is why you don't always see a **wa** or **ga** in each sentence.

26 itsu *(eat-sue)*
when いつ

➡ When is it? いつ です か。
Itsu desu ka? *(eat-sue dess kah)*

27 doko *(doe-koe)*
where どこ

➡ Where is it? どこ です か。
Doko desu ka? *(doe-koe dess kah)*

➡ Where is the bathroom (toilet/washroom)?
おてあらい は どこ です か。
O-tearai wa doko desu ka?
(oh-tay-ah-rai wah doe-koe dess kah)

There are specific words for bathroom and toilet, but the most common general term that is used is **o-tearai** *(oh-tay-ah-rai)* おてあらい. Literally it means "honorable hand wash," (in other words, "wash room").

28 hai *(hi)*
yes はい。

The word **hai** *(hi)* はい does not always simply mean "yes." It can have a variety of meanings, including "I'm listening," or even "Pardon me?" When confirming or agreeing with something, it is better to use **Sō desu** *(soh dess)* そう です, or **Hai, sō desu** *(hi soh dess)* はい、そ う です.

29 **Sō desu.** *(soh dess)*
Yes, that's so, that's right. そう です。

30 **iie** *(eee-eh)*
no いいえ

→ No, that is not correct.
いいえ、そう で は ありません。
Iie, sō de wa arimasen.
(eee-eh soh day wah ah-ree-mah-sen)

The word "no" is not used as much in Japanese as it is in English. Instead, the preferred way of expressing "no" is to use the negative form of the key verb. For example, **ikimasu ka?** *(ee-kee-mah-soo kah)* いきます か meaning "are you going?" is generally answered with the negative **ikimasen** *(ee-kee-mah-sen)* いきませ ん, "I'm not going," rather than **iie** *(eee-eh)* いいえ, a blunt "no."

More Notes on Pronouncing Japanese

Anyone familiar with the pronunciation of Latin, Italian, Spanish, Portuguese, or Hawaiian, has a head start in learning how to pronounce Japanese correctly. In fact, when the sounds of the Japanese language are transcribed into Roman letters (the familiar ABCs), they are pronounced virtually the same as in these languages.

The key to pronouncing Japanese properly is found in the vowels: **a, i, u, e** and **o**. In Japanese the **a** is pronounced as *ah*, the **i** as *ee*, the **u** as *oo*, the **e** as *eh*, the **o** as *oh*—just as in the above languages. For example, **Narita** *(Nah-ree-tah)* なりた, the name of Tokyo's international airport, would be pronounced in a similar way in Spanish, and vice-versa. The Spanish word *"casa"* is pronounced almost the same in both languages, as are *"mesa," "cara," "rio," "Maria,"* and so on.

A significant difference between the pronunciation of Spanish and Japanese words is found in the **L** and **V** sounds. There is no true **L** or **V** sound in Japanese. The **L** comes out as an **R** sound and the **V** as a **B** sound. So "Lolita" in Japanese is **Rorīta** ロリータ; "via" becomes **bia** ビア, etc.

PART 4
Words 31–40

31 iku *(ee-koo)*
to go (plain) いく

ikimasu *(ee-kee-mahss)*
to go (polite neutral) いきます

Japanese verbs are regularly used alone in their present, past, and future tenses as well as in their negative and interrogative forms, as complete sentences. The rest of the meaning is understood from the context.

Japanese verb endings do not change when the subjects change as they do in English. Therefore **ikimasu** *(ee-kee-mahss)* いきます can also mean "I go," "you go," "he goes," "she goes," "it goes," "we go" or "they go."

In the following example sentences only one subject is translated into English for simplicity, but don't forget that a variety of subjects is possible.

Ikimasu. *(ee-kee-mahss)*
I go, I am going. I shall go. いきます。

Ikimasen. *(ee-kee-mah-sen)*
I do not go, I am not going. I shall not go.
いきません。
The plain form is **ikanai** *(ee-kah-nai)* いかない.

Ikimasu ka? *(ee-kee-mahss kah)*
Are you going? いきます か。

Ikimashita. *(ee-kee-mahssh-tah)*
I went. He/she went. いきました。

Ikitai desu. *(ee-kee-tai dess)*
I want to go. いきたい です。

Ikimashō. *(ee-kee-mah-show)*
Let's go. いきましょう。

Itte kudasai. *(eat-tay koo-dah-sai)*
Please go. いって ください。

➡ Where are you going? どこ に いきます か。
Doko ni ikimasu ka? *(doe-koe nee ee-kee-mahss kah)*

➡ Where is he going?
あの ひと は どこ に いきます か。
Ano hito wa doko ni ikimasu ka?
(ah-no ssh-toe wah doe-koe nee ee-kee-mahss kah)

32 hoteru *(hoe-tay-rue)*
hotel ホテル

➡ I want to go to my hotel. ホテル に いきたい です。
Hoteru ni ikitai desu. *(hoe-tay-rue nee ee-kee-tai dess)*

➡ I want to go to the New Otani Hotel.
ニュー オータニ ホテル に いきたい です。
Nyū Ōtani Hoteru ni ikitai desu.
(knew oh-tah-nee hoe-tay-rue nee ee-kee-tai dess)

➡ My hotel is the Miyako Hotel Tokyo.
わたし の ホテル は ミヤコ ホテル とうきょう
です。
Watashi no hoteru wa Miyako Hoteru Tōkyō desu.
(wah-tah-she no hoe-tay-rue wah Me-yah-koe Hoe-tay-rue Tokyo dess)

33 taberu *(tah-bay-rue)*
to eat たべる

Tabemasu. *(tah-bay-mahss)*
I eat (it). I shall eat. I am ready to eat. たべます。

Tabemasu ka? *(tah-bay-mahss kah)*
Will you eat (it)? Do you eat (that)? たべます か

Tabemasen. *(tah-bay-mah-sen)*
I am not going to eat. I do not eat (that). たべません。

Tabemashita. *(tah-bay-mahssh-tah)*
I ate. He/she ate, we ate. たべました。

Tabetai desu. *(tah-bay-tai dess)*
I want to eat. たべたい です。

Tabemashō. *(tah-bay-mah-show)*
Let's eat. たべましょう。

Tabete kudasai. *(tah-bay-tay koo-dah-sai)*
Please eat. たべて ください。

➡ Where do you want to eat?
どこ で たべたい です か。
Doko de tabetai desu ka?
(doe-koe day tah-bay-tai dess kah)

➡ What do you want to eat?
なに を たべたい です か。
Nani o tabetai desu ka? *(nah-nee oh tah-bay-tai dess kah)*

34 shokuji *(show-koo-jee)*
food, meal　しょくじ

➡ Let's (go and) eat. Let's have a meal.
しょくじ を しましょう。
Shokuji o shimashō. *(show-koo-jee oh shee-mah-show)*

35 washoku *(wah-show-koo)*
Japanese food　わしょく

➡ I want to eat Japanese food.
わしょく を たべたい です。
Washoku o tabetai desu.
(wa-show-koo oh tah-bay-tai dess)

As mentioned earlier, **o** *(oh)* を is a grammatical particle used to indicate that the preceding word is the direct object of the sentence.

36 yōshoku *(yoh-show-koo)*
Western food　ようしょく

➡ Let's eat western food.
ようしょく を たべましょう。

Yōshoku o tabemashō.
(yoh-show-koo oh tah-bay-mah-show)

➡ Where shall we eat? どこ で たべましょう か。
Doko de tabemashō ka?
(doe-koe day tah-bay-mah-show kah)

➡ Have you already eaten? もう たべました か。
Mō tabemashita ka? *(moe tah-bay-mahssh-tah kah)*
Mō means "already."

➡ I don't want to eat. たべたくない です。
Tabetaku nai desu.
(tah-bay-tah-koo nai dess)

➡ I don't want to eat Western food.
ようしょく を たべたくない です。
Yōshoku o tabetaku nai desu.
(yoe-show-koo oh tah-bay-tah-koo nai dess)

37 nomu *(no-moo)*
to drink のむ

Nomimasu. *(no-me-mahss)*
I drink. I shall drink. のみます。

Nomimasen. *(no-me-mah-sen)*
I do not drink. I shall not drink. のみません。

This phase may also be used for "I don't want anything to drink."

Nomimasu ka? *(no-me-mahss ka)*
Will you (have a) drink? のみます か。

Mō nomimashita. *(mo no-me-mahssh-tah)*
I drank (already). もう のみました。

Nomitai desu. *(no-me-tai dess)*
I want to drink. のみたい です。

Nomimashō. *(no-me-mah-show)*
Let's drink. のみましょう。

Nonde kudasai. *(noan-day koo-dah-sai)*
Please drink. のんで ください。

Nomanai de kudasai. *(no-mah-nai day koo-dah-sai)*
Please don't drink. のまないで ください。

➡ Would you like something to drink?
なにか のみたい です か。
Nani ka nomitai desu ka?
(nah-nee kah no-me-tai dess kah)
Putting **ka** *(kah)* か after **nani** *(nah-nee)* なに changes
the meaning from "what" to "something."

➡ I'd like to drink a cola. コーラ を のみたい です。
Kōra o nomitai desu. *(koe-rah oh no-me-tai dess)*

➡ I'd like (to drink) a beer. ビール を のみたい です。
Bīru o nomitai desu. *(bee-rue oh no-me-tai dess)*

➡ I do not drink sake. さけ を のみません。
Sake o nomimasen. *(sah-kay oh no-me-mah-sen)*

Nomitakunai desu. *(no-me-tah-ku nai dess)*
I don't want to drink / I don't want anything to drink. のみたくない　です。

38 suki *(ski)*
like (be fond of, love)　すき

➡ Do you like sushi? すし　が　すき　です　か。
Sushi ga suki desu ka? *(sue-she gah ski dess kah)*

➡ I don't like it. すき　で　は　ありません。
Suki de wa arimasen. *(ski de wah ah-ree-mah-sen)*

➡ I want (would like) to eat sushi.
すし　を　たべたい　です。
Sushi o tabetai desu. *(sue-she oh tah-bay-tai dess)*

➡ I don't like that.
それ　が　すき　で　は　ありません。
Sore ga suki de wa arimasen.
(soe-ray gah ski day wah ah-ree-mah-sen)

➡ I like this. これ　が　すき　です。
Kore ga suki desu. *(koe-ray gah ski dess)*

➡ I don't like this. これ　が　すき　で　は　ありません。
Kore ga suki de wa arimasen.
(koe-ray gah ski day wah ah-ree-mah-sen)

➡ I don't like whiskey.
ウィスキー　が　すき　で　は　ありません。

Uisukī ga suki de wa arimasen.
(oo-iss-key gah ski day wah ah-ree-mah-sen)

39 Itadakimasu *(ee-tah-dah-kee-mahss)*
to receive, accept いただきます。

This expression is invariably said just before beginning a meal (particularly when you are a guest). The literal meaning of it is "I receive/accept (this food)." In general this is also a formal, polite way of expressing appreciation and thanks. Prior to taking the first drink, the traditional Japanese salutation is **kampai!** *(kahm-pai)* かんぱい、"Cheers!"

Gochisōsama deshita *(go-chee-soh-sah-mah desh-tah)*
Thank you for the meal (or drinks).

ごちそうさま でした。

This is a formal and common way of expressing thanks and appreciation to the person who has prepared, hosted, or paid for a meal or drinks.

40 oishii *(oh-ee-she-e)*
(it is) delicious おいしい

➡ Is it good? おいしい です か。
Oishii desu ka? *(oh-ee-she-e dess kah)*

Oishikatta desu. *(oh-ee-she-kaht-tah dess)*
(It was) delicious. おいしかった です。

Those Kanji Characters!

Originally the Japanese imported over 60,000 Chinese characters **kanji**, *(kahn-jee)* かんじ, but only a small percentage of this number is commonly used today. Successive language reforms that began in Japan shortly after the fall of the Tokugawa shogunate in 1868 have greatly reduced the number of **kanji** taught in schools and used for official purposes.

In 1981 the number of characters was officially set at 1,945. This list is referred to as the **Jōyō Kanji** *(joe-yoh kahn-jee)* じょうようかんじ or "Chinese Characters in General Use." The last major reform occurred in 1989, when the total number of characters children are required to learn during their first six years of school was increased to 1,006.

PART 5
Words 41–50

41 **au** *(ah-oo)*
to meet あう

Remember that subjects are often unexpressed in Japanese. The following sentences are translated into English using the subject "I," but could also be understood to mean "he," "she," "they," "we," "it," "that person," and so forth.

Aimasu. *(eye-mahss)*
I shall meet (someone). あいます。

Aimasen. *(eye-mah-sen)*
I shall not meet (someone). あいません。

Aimasu ka? *(eye-mahss kah)*
Will you meet me? あいます か。

(Person's name)-san ni aimashita.
(... -sahn nee eye-mahssh-tah)
I met (person's name). …さん に あいました。

Aitai desu. *(eye-tai dess)*
I want to meet (you). あいたい です。

Aimashō. *(eye-mah show)*
Let's meet. あいましょう。

➡ Where shall we meet?
どこ　で　あいましょう　か。
Doko de aimashō ka?
(doe-koe day eye-mah-show kah)
The word preceding the particle **de** *(day)* で often indicates a place where the action of the verb happens.

➡ Please meet me at the hotel. ホテル　で　あいましょう。
Hoteru de aimashō.
(Hoe-tay-rue day eye-mah-show)

➡ Please meet me in the lobby. Let's meet in the lobby.
ロビー　で　あいましょう。
Robī de aimashō. *(roe-bee day eye-mah-show)*

42 nanji ? *(nahn-jee)*
what time? なんじ

➡ What time shall we meet?
なんじ　に　あいましょう　か。
Nanji ni aimashō ka?
(nahn-jee nee eye-mah-show kah)

➡ Where shall we meet tonight?
こんばん　どこ　で　あいましょう　か。
Komban doko de aimashō ka?
(kone-bahn doe-koe day eye-mah-show kah)

➡ What time do you want to go?
なんじ　に　いきたい　です　か。
Nanji ni ikitai desu ka?
(nahn-jee nee ee-kee-tai dess kah)

➡ What time do you eat? What time are we going to eat?
なんじ に たべます か。
Nanji ni tabemasu ka? *(nahn-jee nee tah-bay-mahss kah)*

➡ When shall we meet?　いつ　あいましょう　か。
Itsu aimashō ka? *(eat-sue eye-mah-show kah)*

43 aru *(ah-rue)*
to be, have (for objects)　ある

Arimasu. *(ah-ree-mahss)*
There is. There are. I have.　あります。

Arimasen. *(ah-ree-mah-sen)*
There is not. There are not. I do not have (it, any).
ありません。

Arimashita. *(ah-ree-mahssh-tah)*
There was. There were. I had.　ありました。

➡ Do you have some (any/it)? Is there any?
あります　か。
Arimasu ka? *(ah-ree-mahss kah)*

➡ No, I don't have any (it). There is none.　ありません。
Arimasen. *(ah-ree-mah-sen)*

44 ikura *(ee-koo-rah)*
how much　いくら

➡ How much is it?　いくら　です　か。
Ikura desu ka? *(ee-koo-rah dess kah)*

How much is this? これ は いくら です か。
Kore wa ikura desu ka?
(koe-ray wah ee-koo-rah dess kah)

➡ How much is that? それ は いくら です か。
Sore wa ikura desu ka?
(soe-ray wah ee-koo-rah dess kah)

45 takai *(tah-kai)*
high, expensive　たかい

➡ That is expensive. それ は たかい です。
Sore wa takai desu. *(soe-ray wah tah-kai dess)*

46 yasui *(yah-sue-e)*
cheap, inexpensive　やすい

➡ Do you have a cheap one?
やすい の は あります か。
Yasui no wa arimasu ka?
(yah-sue-e no wah ah-ree-mahss kah)

47 suru *(sue-rue)*
to do　する

Shimasu. *(she-mahss)*
I do (it). I shall do. I am going to do.　します。

Shimasen. *(she-mah-sen)*
I do not do (it). I shall not do. I am not going to do.　しません。

Shimasu ka? *(she-mahss kah)*
Do you do (it)? Will you do?　します　か。

Shimashita. *(she-mahss-tah)*
I did (it).　しました。

Shitai desu. *(she-tai dess)*
I want to do (it).　したい　です。

Shimashō. *(she-mah-show)*
Let's do (it).　しましょう。

Shite kudasai. *(she-tay koo-dah-sai)*
Please do (it).　して　ください。

Shinaide kudasai. *(she-nai day koo-dah-sai)*
Please don't do (it).　しないで　ください。

➡ What shall we do?　なに　を　しましょう　か。
   Nani o shimashō ka? *(nah-nee oh she-mah-show kah)*

➡ What are you doing?　なに　を　して　います　か。
   Nani o shite imasu ka?
   (nah-nee oh ssh-tay ee-mahss kah)

   Shite imasu *(ssh-tay ee-mahss)*（して　います）is the present progressive form of **shimasu**, which changes "do" into "doing."

➡ What are you (we) going to do? What shall we do?
   どう　します　か。
   Dō shimasu ka? *(doh she-mahss kah)*

➡ How should it be done? / How should I do it?
どう いう ふう に しますか。
Dō iu fū ni shimasu ka? *(doh yoo fuu nee she-mahss kah)*

Dō *(doh)* どう can mean "what," "how," or "why,"
depending on the usage. **Dō iu fū ni** *(doh yoo fuu nee)*
どういうふうに means "How," "In what manner."

➡ What is he (it/that person) doing?
あの ひと は なに を して います か。
Ano hito wa nani o shite imasu ka?
(ah-no ssh-toe wah nah-nee oh ssh-tay ee-mahss kah)

➡ What do you want to do? なに を したい です か。
Nani o shitai desu ka? *(nah-nee oh she-tai dess kah)*

➡ I don't want to do anything. なにも したくない です。
Nani mo shitakunai desu.
(nah-nee moe she-tah-koo nai dess)

➡ What did you do? なにをしましたか。
Nani o shimashita ka? *(nah-nee oh she-mahssh-tah kah)*

➡ I didn't do anything. なにも しません でした。
Nanimo shimasen deshita.
(nah-nee moe she-mah-sen desh-tah)

48 ii *(eee)*
good (fine, acceptable) いい

➡ Is it okay? いい です か。
Ii desu ka? *(eee dess kah)*

➡ Is this okay? これ は いい です か。

Kore wa ii desu ka? *(koe-ray wah eee dess kah)*

➡ That's fine. それ　は　いい　です。
Sore wa ii desu. *(soe-ray wah eee dess)*

➡ Is it okay to go? いって　も　いい　です　か。
Itte mo ii desu ka? *(eat-tay moe eee dess kah)*

Itte *(eat-tay)* いって is the so-called "*te*-form" form of the verb **ikimasu** (meaning go) that by itself is a command. **Mo ii desu ka?** *(moe eee dess kah)* …も　いい　です　か after the "*te*-form" of a verb adds the sense of "May I… ?" or "Is it alright to…?"

➡ Is it okay to eat? たべて　も　いい　です　か。
Tabete mo ii desu ka? *(tah-bay-tay moe eee dess kah)*

➡ Is it okay to do it? して　も　いい　です　か。
Shite mo ii desu ka? *(ssh-tay moe eee dess kah)*

➡ What time are we (you) going?
なんじ　に　いきます　か。
Nanji ni ikimasu ka? *(nahn-jee nee ee-kee-mahs kah)*

49 dochira *(doe-chee-rah)*
which (of two) どちら

➡ Which one (of these two) is the best?
どちら　が　いい　です　か。
Dochira ga ii desu ka? *(doe-chee-rah gah eee dess kah)*

➡ Which one is the more expensive (out of these two)?
どちら　が　たかい　です　か。

Dochira ga takai desu ka?
(doe-chee-rah gah tah-kai dess kah)

50 dore *(doe-ray)*
which (of many) どれ

→ Which one (out of all of them) is yours?
どれ　が　…さん　の　です　か。
Dore ga (person's name)-san no desu ka?
(doe-ray gah…-sahn no dess kah)

Writing Japanese "English"

The earliest Western visitors to Japan faced an enormous challenge in trying to learn the Japanese language because it was written in a script they could not pronounce. Several of the more scholarly inclined of these early visitors created phonetic systems based on the familiar ABCs for writing the language. Unfortunately, each of these systems was designed for speakers of a specific language (Portuguese, Dutch, German, English), and was therefore not universally applicable to all foreigners wanting to learn Japanese.

Finally, an American medical missionary named Dr. James Curtis Hepburn, who went to Japan in 1859 after earlier spending fourteen years in Singapore and Amoy, collaborated in the development of a system for romanizing Japanese that was eventually to become the standard. This is known as the "Hepburn System of Romanization."

While in Japan, Dr. Hepburn also helped found Meiji Gakuin University and served as its first president. His publication in 1867 of *A Japanese-English Dictionary*, the first such dictionary, played a key role in introducing Japan to the outside world. Dr. Hepburn returned to the U.S. in 1892 and died in 1911.

Some Japanese educators and scholars did not appreciate the fact that a foreigner had played a leading role in the development of **Rōmaji**, and came up with a number of systems based on Japanese perspectives. But these systems did not win popular support because foreigners could not pronounce many of the Romanized syllables correctly.

The Hepburn System is used in Japan by most government and private institutions, and almost exclusively outside of Japan.

The main reason that the Japanese romanizing systems have not succeeded in competing with or replacing the Hepburn system is because they make use of Chinese style romanization in which several sounds are represented by letters that are quite different from their use in English and the Romance languages of Europe. For example, **ti** stands for the sound *chi*, **tu** for the sound *tsu*, **z** for *j*, and so on.

PART 6
Words 51–60

51 chiisai *(chee-e-sai)*
small, littler　ちいさい

➡ I like the small one.　ちいさい　の　は　すき　です。
Chiisai no wa suki desu. *(chee-e-sai no wah ski dess)*

➡ Which one is the smaller (out of these two)?
どちら　が　ちいさい　です　か。
Dochira ga chiisai desu ka?
(doe-chee-rah gah chee-e-sai dess kah)

➡ This is too small.　これ　は　ちいさすぎます。
Kore wa chiisa-sugimasu.
(koe-ray wah chee-e-sah sue-ghee-mahss)

➡ I shall take the small one.
ちいさい　の　を　いただきます。
Chiisai no o itadakimasu.
(chee-e-sai no oh ee-tah-dah-kee-mahss)

52 ōkii *(oh-kee-e)*
large, big　おおきい

➡ Do you have a bigger one?
もっと　おおきい　の　は　あります　か。
Motto ōkii no wa arimasu ka?
(mote-toe oh-kee-e no wah ah-ree-mahss kah)

Motto adds the meaning of more; in this example it is
literally "more big," meaning "larger" or "bigger."

➡ Do you have a smaller one?
もっと ちいさい の は あります か。
Motto chiisai no wa arimasu ka?
(mote-toe chee-e-sai no wah ah-ree-mahss kah)

53 ichiban *(ee-chee-bahn)*
number one, most いちばん

When used before adjectives, the phrase **ichiban** *(ee-chee-bahn)* いちばん marks the superlative form ("-est", as in "biggest", "best", "cheapest").

➡ Which one is the cheapest?
どれ が いちばん やすい です か。
Dore ga ichiban yasui desu ka?
(doe-ray gah ee-chee-bahn yah-sue-ee dess kah)

➡ Which one is the best?
どれ が いちばん いい です か。
Dore ga ichiban ii desu ka?
(doe-ray gah ee-chee-bahn eee dess kah)

➡ Which one do you prefer?
どれ が すき です か。
Dore ga suki desu ka? *(doe-ray gah ski dess kah)*

➡ I shall take that one. How much is it?
それ を ください。いくら です か。
Sore o kudasai. Ikura desu ka?
(soe-ray oh koo-dah-sai, ee-koo-rah dess kah)

54 dasu *(dah-sue)*
to send, mail だす

The verb ***dasu** (dah-sue)* だす has a general meaning of "to put out," "to take out". It is often used to express "posting a letter or parcel."

Dashimasu. *(dah-she-mahss)*
I shall mail (it). だします。

Dashimasen. *(dah-she-mah-sen)*
I do not send (it). I shall not send (it). だしません。

Dashimashita. *(dah-she-mahssh-tah)*
I sent (it). I mailed it. だしました。

Dashitai desu. *(dah-she-tai dess)*
I want to mail (this). だしたい　です。

Dashite kudasai. *(dah-ssh-tah koo-dah-sai)*
Please send (this). Please mail (it).
だして　ください。

➡ Please mail this today.
これ　を　きょう　だして　ください。
Kore o kyō dashite kudasai.
(koe-ray oh k'yoe dah-ssh-tah koo-dah-sai)

55 koko *(koe-koe)*
here ここ

➡ Let's have something to drink here.
ここで　なにか　のみましょう。
Koko de nani ka nomimashō.
(koe-koe day nah-nee kah no-me-mah-show)

➡ Where am I? (literally: Where is this?)
ここ　は　どこ　ですか。
Koko wa doko desu ka?
(koe-koe wah doe-koe dess kah)

➡ Is this place Okay? ここ は いい です か。
Koko wa ii desu ka? *(koe-koe wah eee dess kah)*

56 tomaru *(toe-mah-rue)*
to stop (come to rest). To stay (overnight). とまる

Tomarimasu. *(toe-mah-ree-mahss)*
I stop. I shall stop. It (the train, etc.) stops. I shall stay (overnight). とまります。

Tomarimasen. *(toe-mah-ree-mah-sen)*
I do not stop. I shall not stop. It does not stop. I shall not stay (overnight). とまりません。

Tomarimashita. *(toe-mah-ree-mahssh-tah)*
I/It stopped. I stayed (overnight). とまりました。

Tomarimasu ka? *(toe-mah-ree-mahssh kah)*
Do you stop? Will you/it stop? Will you stay (overnight)? とまります か。

Tomaritai desu. *(toe-mah-ree-tai dess)*
I want to stop. I want to stay (overnight).
とまりたい です。

Tomarimashō. *(toe-mah-ree-mah-show)*
Let's stop. Let's stay. とまりましょう。

Tomatte kudasai. *(toe-mah-tay koo-dah-sai)*
Please stop. とまって ください。

➡ Please stop here. ここ　で　とまって　ください。
Koko de tomatte kudasai.
(koe-koe day toe-mah-tay koo-dah-sai)

➡ I want (you) to stop here. ここ　で　とまりたい　です。
Koko de tomaritai desu.
(koe-koe day toe-mah-ree-tai dess)

➡ Where shall we stop? どこ　で　とまりましょう　か。
Doko de tomarimashō ka?
(doe-koe day toe-mah-ree-mah-show kah)

➡ Where are we staying tonight?
こんばん　どこ　に　とまります　か。
Konban doko ni tomarimasu ka?
(kome-bahn doe-koe nee toe-mah-ree-mahss kah)

Konban *(kome-bahn)* こんばん (tonight) is the same **komban** that you saw earlier in **komban wa**, which means "good evening." You can use **komban wa** as soon as it's dark.

57 matsu *(maht-sue)*
to wait まつ

Machimasu. *(mah-chee-mahss)*
I shall wait. まちます。

Machimasen. *(mah-chee-mah-sen)*
I shall not wait. まちません。

Machimasu ka? *(mah-chee-mahss kah)*
Will you wait? まちますか。

Machimashita. *(mah-chee-mahss-tah)*
I waited. He/She waited. まちました。

Machitai desu. *(mah-chee-tai dess)*
I want to wait. まちたい です。

Machimashō *(mah-chee-mah-show)*
Let's wait. まちましょう。

Matte kudasai. *(maht-tay koo-dah-sai)*
Please wait. まって ください。

➡ I shall wait for you here.
ここ で まちます。
Koko de machimasu. *(koe-koe day mah-chee-mahss)*

Wait here. ここ で まって ください。
Koko de matte kudasai.
(koe-koe day maht-tay koo-dah-sai)

➡ I shall wait at the hotel. ホテル で まちます。
Hoteru de machimasu. *(hoe-tay-rue day mah-chee-mahss)*

➡ I shall wait in my room. へや で まちます。
Heya de machimasu. *(hay-yah day mah-chee-mahss)*

➡ Is it okay if I wait here?
ここ で まって も いい です か?
Koko de matte mo ii desu ka?
(koe-koe day maht-tay moe eee dess kah)

➡ Please don't wait. またないで ください。
Matanaide kudasai. *(mah-tah-nai day koo-dah-sai)*

47

58 kuru *(koo-rue)*
to come くる

Kimasu. *(kee-mahss)*
I shall come. He/She will come. きます。

Kimasen. *(kee-mah-sen)*
I shall not come. He/She will not come. きません。

Kimasu ka? *(kee-mahss kah)*
Will you come? Are you coming? きます か。

Kimashita. *(kee-mahssh-tah)*
I /He/She came. きました。

Kite kudasai. *(kee-tay koo-dah-sai)*
Please come. きて ください。

➡ Is he coming here? Are you coming here?
ここ に きます か。
Koko ni kimasu ka?
(koe-koe nee kee-mahss kah)

➡ Is she coming this afternoon? Are you coming this afternoon? きょう の ごご に きます か。
Kyō no gogo ni kimasu ka?
(k'yoe no go-go nee kee-mahss kah)

➡ I am not coming. They are not coming. She/He is not
coming. きません。
Kimasen. *(kee-mah-sen)*

59 kau *(kah-oo)*
to buy かう

Kaimasu. *(kai-mahss)*
I shall buy (it). かいます。

Kaimasen. *(kai-mah-sen)*
I shall not buy (it). かいません。

Kaimasu ka? *(kai-mahss kah)*
Will you buy (it)? Are you going to buy (it)?
かいます　か。

Kaimashita. *(kai-mahssh-tah)*
I bought (it). He/She bought (it) かいました。

Kaitai desu. *(kai-tai dess)*
I want to buy (this). かいたいです。

Kaimashō. *(kai-mah-show)*
Let's buy (it). かいましょう。

Katte kudasai. *(kaht-tay koo-dah-sai)*
Please buy (it). かって　ください。

➡ I want to buy that. それ　を　かいたい　です。
Sore o kaitai desu. *(sore-ray oh kai-tai dess)*

➡ What do you want to buy?
なに　を　かいたい　です　か。
Nani o kaitai desu ka? *(nah-nee oh kai-tai dess kah)*

➡ Please buy it for me. わたし　に　かって　ください。
Watashi ni katte kudasai.
(wah-tah-shee nee kaht-tay koo-dah-sai)

➡ Where did you buy that?
それ　を　どこ　で　かいました　か。
Sore o doko de kaimashita ka?
(soe-ray oh doe-koe day kai-mahssh-tah kah)

➡ Did you buy this at a department store?
これ　を　デパート　で　かいました　か。
Kore o depāto de kaimashita ka?
(koe-ray oh day-pah-to day kai-mahssh-tah kah)

➡ What did you buy? なに　を　かいました　か。
Nani o kaimashita ka?
(nah-nee oh kai-mahssh-tah kah)

60 kaimono *(kai-moe-no)*
shopping かいもの

➡ I want to go shopping. かいもの　に　いきたい　です。
Kaimono ni ikitai desu.
(kei-moe-no nee ee-kee-tai dess)

➡ Let's go shopping. かいもの　に　いきましょう。
Kaimono ni ikimashō.
(kai-moe-no nee ee-kee-mah show)

➡ Did you go shopping? かいもの　に　いきました　か。
Kaimono ni ikimashita ka?
(kai-moe-no nee ee-kee-mahssh-tah kah)

I like shopping. かいもの　が　すき　です。
Kaimono ga suki desu! *(kai-moe-no gah ski dess)*

Dealing with Japanized English

Some 25,000 foreign words, mostly from English, have been merged into the Japanese language, and are now as commonly used as native Japanese terms. But this massive adoption of English vocabulary has not made it much easier for non-Japanese speaking people to understand or learn the language.

The reason for this rather odd problem is that all of the adopted English words are written and pronounced according to Japanese pronunciation. That is, each word is broken up into Japanese syllables that are then written or pronounced in the normal Japanese way. This means that a simple English word like "strike" becomes **sutoraiki** *(sue-toe-rey-kee)* ストライキ, "milk" becomes **miruku** *(miruku)* ミルク, "blue" becomes **burū** *(boo-rue)* ブルー, "sex" becomes **sekkusu** *(say-koo-sue)* セックス—all of which are absolutely meaningless to a native English speaker until the meanings of the words are explained—or unless the foreigner is familiar enough with this Japanization process to convert it back to English automatically.

Other foreign words are abbreviated as they are Japanized, making them even harder to understand. A recent news issue is that of **sekuhara**, which means "sexual harassment" and was created by combining the first parts of the two English words.

When Japanized English words are used by themselves, or in abbreviated contexts in which the meaning is not obvious, they are like any other foreign language that one has to learn in order to understand.

My daughter Demetra, who spent six months in Tokyo studying Japanese, went shopping one day and was stumped for hours by the term **berubetto** *(bay-rye-bait-toe)* ベルベット. A bi-lingual girlfriend solved the mystery for her—velvet!

PART 7
Words 61–70

61 o-kane (*oh-kah-nay*)
money おかね

→ Is this your money?
   これ は …さん の おかね です か。
   Kore wa (person's name)-san no o-kane desu ka?
   (*koe-ray wah… -sahn no oh-kah-nay dess kah*)

→ Yes, it is. はい、そう です。
   Hai, sō desu. (*hi, soh dess*)

62 motsu (*moat-sue*)
to have もつ

   Motte imasu. (*moat-tay e-mahss*)
   I/He/She/They have. もって います。

   Motte imasen. (*moat-tay e-mah-sen*)
   I do not have. もって いません。

→ Do you have any Japanese money?
   にほん の おかね を もって います か。
   Nihon no o-kane o motte imasu ka?
   (*nee-hone no oh-kah-nay o moat-tay e-mahss kah*)

→ No, I don't (have any). もって いません。
   Motte imasen. (*moat-tay-e-mah-sen*)

➡ Do you have any dollars?
ドル を もって います か。
Doru o motte imasu ka?
(doe-rue oh moat-tay ee-mahss kah)

➡ Yes, I have. もって います。
Motte imasu. *(moat-tay ee-mahss)*

➡ What do you have?
なに を もって います か。
Nani o motte imasu ka?
(nah-nee oh moat-tay ee-mahss kah)

63 yobu *(yoe-boo)*
to call (out to someone, call a taxi, etc.) よぶ

Yobimasu. *(yoe-bee-mahss)*
I shall call (someone). よびます。

Yobimasen. *(yoe-bee-mah-sen)*
I do not call. I shall not call. よびません。

Yobimasu ka? *(yoe-bee-mahss kah)*
Will you call? よびます か。

Yobimashita. *(yoe-bee-mahssh-tah)*
I called. よびました。

Yobimashō. *(yoe-bee-mah-show)*
Let's call (someone). よびましょう。

(person's name) -san o yonde kudasai...
(...sahn oh yoan-day koo-dah-sai)
Please call (person's name).
…さん を よんで ください。

➡ Did you call me? よびました か。
Yobimashita ka? *(yoe-bee-mahssh-tah kah)*

➡ Who called me?
どなた が わたし を よびました か。
Donata ga watashi o yobimashita ka?
(doe-nah-tah gah wah-tah-she oh yoe-bee-mahssh-tah kah)

64 denwa *(den-wah)*
telephone でんわ

Denwa o shimasu. *(den-wah oh she-mahss)*
I shall telephone (you/him/her/the company)
でんわ を します。

Denwa o shimashita. *(den-wah oh she-mahssh-tah)*
I/He/She telephoned. でんわ を しました。

Denwa o shimasen. *(den-wah oh she-mah-sen)*
I do not telephone. I shall not telephone.
でんわ を しません。

Denwa o shimasen deshita.
(den-wah oh she-mah-sen dessh-tah)
I did not call. He/She did not call.
でんわ を しません でした。

Denwa o shitai desu. *(den-wah oh she-tai dess)*
I want to telephone. I want to make a call.
でんわ を したい です。

Denwa o shimashō. *(den-wah oh she-mah-show)*
Let's telephone. でんわ を しましょう。

➡ Was there a telephone call (for me)?
でんわ が ありました か。
Denwa ga arimashita ka?
(den-wah gah ah-ree-mahssh-tah kah)

➡ Please telephone me. でんわ を して ください。
Denwa o shite kudasai. *(den-wah oh she-tay koo-dah-sai)*

➡ Please telephone him (her).
あの ひと に でんわ を して ください。
Ano hito ni denwa o shite kudasai.
(ah-no ssh-toe nee den-wah oh ssh-tay koo-dah-sai)

➡ Please telephone my hotel.
わたし の ホテル に でんわ を して ください。
Watashi no hoteru ni denwa o shite kudasai.
(wah-tah-she no hoe-tay-rue nee den-wah oh ssh-tay koo-dah-sai)

➡ Mr. Smith, telephone (for you).
スミスさん、でんわ です。
Sumisu-san, denwa desu.
(sue-me-sue-sahn, den-wah dess)

➡ Who is the telephone call for?
でんわ は どなた に です か。
Denwa wa donata ni desu ka?
(den-wah wah doe-nah-tah nee dess kah)

65 kaku *(kah-koo)*
to write かく

Kakimasu. *(kah-kee-mahss)*
I write. I shall write. かきます。

Kakimasen. *(kah-kee-mah-sen)*
I do not write. I shall not write. かきません。

Kakimasen deshita. *(kah-kee-mah-sen dessh-tah)*
I did not write. かきません　でした。

Kakimasu ka? *(kah-kee-mahss kah)*
Do you write? Will you write? かきます　か。

Kakimashita. *(kah-kee-mahssh-tah)*
I/He/She wrote. かきました。

➡ I want to write a book.
ほん　を　かきたい　です。
Hon o kakitai desu. *(hone oh kah-kee-tai dess)*

➡ Please write your name here.
ここ　に　なまえ　を　かいて　ください。
Koko ni namae o kaite kudasai.
(koe-koe nee nah-my oh kai-tay koo-dah-sai)

➡ Where do I write my name?
なまえ　を　どこ　に　かきます　か。
Namae o doko ni kakimasu ka?
(nah-my oh doe-koe nee kah-kee-mahss kah)

56

➡ It is written down. かいて　あります。
Kaite arimasu. *(kai-tay ah-ree-mahss)*

➡ Please write it down. かいて　ください。
Kaite kudasai. *(kai-tay koo-dah-sai)*

66 dekiru *(day-kee-rue)*
to be able to do, can do できる

Dekimasu. *(day-kee-mahss)*
I can do (it). できます。

Dekimasen. *(day-kee-mah-sen)*
I cannot do (it). できません。

Dekimasu ka? *(day-kee-mahss kah)*
Can you/he/she do (it)? できますか。

Dekimashita. *(day-kee-mahssh-tah)*
I/He/She did (it). できました。

➡ Can you do something (about it)?
なに か　できます　か。
Nanika dekimasu ka?
(nah-nee kah day-kee-mahss kah)

➡ Can you do it? できますか。
Dekimasu ka? *(day-kee-mahss kah)*

➡ I/He/She cannot do it. できません。
Dekimasen. *(day-kee-mah-sen)*

➡ I/He/She cannot do anything (about it).
なにも　できません。
Nanimo dekimasen. *(nah-nee moe day-kee-mah-sen)*

67 kyō *(k'yoe)*
today きょう

➡ Can you do it today? きょう　できます　か。
Kyō dekimasu ka? *(k'yoe day-kee-mahss kah)*

Remember *iku (ee-koo)* いく, meaning "to go?"

Ikimasu *(ee-kee-mahss)*
I/He/She is going. いきます。

➡ Where are you/we/they going today?
きょう　どこ　に　いきます　か。
Kyō doko ni ikimasu ka?
(k'yoe doe-koe nee ee-kee-mahss kah)

➡ Today I'm (we're/they're) not going anywhere.
きょう　どこ　に　も　いきません。
Kyō doko ni mo ikimasen.
(k'yoe doe-koe nee moe ee-kee-mah-sen)

68 ashita *(ahssh-tah)*
tomorrow あした

➡ Can you do it by tomorrow?
あした　まで　に　できます　か。
Ashita made ni dekimasu ka?
(ahssh-tah mah-day nee day-kee-mahss kah)

Made *(mah-day)* まで means "until," but **made ni**
(mah-day nee) までに means "by."

58

➡ Where would you like to go tomorrow?
あした どこ に いきたい です か。
Ashita doko ni ikitai desu ka?
(ahssh-tah doe-koe nee ee-kee-tai dess kah)

69 Eigo *(a-e-go)*
English えいご

Pronounce the **ei** of **eigo** like "a" in the familiar ABCs, or as in "hay."

➡ Can you speak (literally: "do") English?
えいご が できます か。
Eigo ga dekimasu ka? *(a-e-go gah day-kee-mahss kah)*

70 Nihongo *(nee-hone-go)*
Japanese にほんご

➡ I cannot speak (literally: "cannot do") Japanese.
にほんご が できません。
Nihongo ga dekimasen.
(nee-hone-go gah day-kee-mah-sen)

Levels of Politeness in Japanese

Japanese, like a number of other languages, has more than one level of polite speech that involves vocabulary, word endings, and even a change in tone and physical posture. Among friends and family the so-called "plain form" is used, but for situations outside these immediate circles, the Japanese normally use the "polite-neutral" form. This is also the appropriate level to be used by for non-Japanese in most situations.

Unless otherwise indicated, all phrases in this book are presented in the polite-neutral form. For very formal occasions, ultra-polite forms of Japanese are used. These are referred to as **keigo** *(kay-e-go)* けいご, which is generally translated as "honorifics," in reference to "high level" Japanese people. Humble Japanese, which you use when referring to yourself, is also a kind of **keigo**. On the ultra-polite level, "to be" (**desu**) becomes **de gozaimasu** *(day go-zai-mahss)* で ございます.

There are many other extremely polite forms and words. For example, there are three different words for "say": the humble **mōsu** *(moe-sue)* もうす, the standard **iu** *(yoo)* いう, and the ultra-polite **ossharu** *(oh-shah-rue)* おっしゃる. Adding **o-** or **go-** before some nouns, adjectives and adverbs makes them (and your speech) extra polite. Japan's famous rice wine, **sake** *(sah-kay)* さけ is often called **o-sake** *(oh-sah-kay)* おさけ.

Japan's different levels of speech developed because of a feudal social system in which rank was expressed by both speech forms and rituals, including kneeling or sitting on the floor and bowing. The level of speech that was appropriate in any situation was determined by the social positions of the people involved. Age and gender were also key elements.

The physical etiquette and manner of speaking developed by the ruling samurai class was so precise and comprehensive that it took years to learn and required constant attention for it to be performed properly. Failure to speak in an accepted manner to a superior was a very serious offense. In some cases it could result in the death penalty.

Women, especially older women, will normally use a higher level of speech than men even in ordinary circumstances. In informal situations, men (except those who are highly cultured) commonly use a rougher, coarser level of Japanese that may sound like a dialect to untutored ears. A number of Japan's traditional occupations, such as that of the

geisha *(gay-e-sha)* げいしゃ, have thier own language with a distinctive vocabulary and ways of speaking.

The ubiquitous -**san** *(sahn)* さん that is attached to the end of names is the equivalent of Mr., Mrs., or Miss. It is very important to use -**san** even in situations calling for ordinary, polite speech because not using it may be considered rude, insulting, arrogant, or worse. However, you should note that honorific prefixes and words are generally not used when referring to oneself or one's family members. For example, you should never introduce yourself as "So & So-san."

PART 8
Words 71–80

71 ikutsu *(ee-koot-sue)*
how many　いくつ

➡ How many do you have? How many are there?
いくつ　あります　か。
Ikutsu arimasu ka?
(ee-koot-sue ah-ree-mass kah)

72 iru *(ee-rue)*
to need, want　いる

Irimasu. *(ee-ree-mahss)*
I need (something).　いります。

Irimasen. *(ee-ree-mah-sen)*
I don't need (it).　いりません。

Irimasu ka? *(ee-ree-mahss kah)*
Do you need (it)?　いります　か。

Irimashita. *(ee-ree-mahssh-tah)*
I needed (it).　いりました。

➡ How many do you need? How many do you want?
いくつ　いります　か。
Ikutsu irimasu ka?
(ee-koot-sue ee-ree-mahss kah)

➡ Do you need this? Do you want this?
これ が いります か。
Kore ga irimasu ka? *(koe-ray gah ee-ree-mahss kah)*

➡ I don't want it. I don't need it. いりません。
Irimasen. *(ee-ree-mah-sen)*

73 wakaru *(wah-kah-rue)*
to understand, to know, to be clear わかる

Wakarimasu. *(wah-kah-ree-mahss)*
I know. わかります。

Wakarimasen. *(wah-kah-ree-mah-sen)*
I do not understand. I don't know. わかりません。

Wakarimasu ka? *(wah-kah-ree-mahss kah)*
Do you understand? わかります か。

Wakarimashita. *(wah-kah-ree-mahssh-tah)*
I (have) understood. I understand. わかりました。

➡ Did you understand (me)? わかりました か。
Wakarimashita ka? *(wah-kah-ree-mahssh-tah kah)*

➡ I did not understand. わかりません でした。
Wakarimasen deshita. *(wah-kah-ree-mah-sen dessh-tah)*

➡ Do you know her name?
あの ひと の なまえ が わかります か。
Ano hito no namae ga wakarimasu ka?
(ah-no-ssh-toe no nah-may gah wah-kah-ree-mahss kah)

→ No, I don't know (it). わかりません。
Wakarimasen. *(wah-kah-ree-mah-sen)*

74 ban/bangō *(bahn/bahn-go)*
number/numbers ばん／ばんごう

There are two sets of numbers in Japanese. One set
(made up of original Japanese terms) goes only from
one through ten. The other set, which was adopted from
China, is complete.

JAPANESE NUMBERS

1	**hitotsu** *(he-toe-t'sue)*	ひとつ
2	**futatsu** *(fuu-tah-t'sue)*	ふたつ
3	**mittsu** *(meet-sue)*	みっつ
4	**yottsu** *(yoat-sue)*	よっつ
5	**itsutsu** *(eat-sue-t'sue)*	いつつ
6	**muttsu** *(moot-sue)*	むっつ
7	**nanatsu** *(nah-nah-t'sue)*	ななつ
8	**yattsu** *(yaht-sue)*	やっつ
9	**kokonotsu** *(koe-koe-no-t'sue)*	ここのつ
10	**tō** *(toe)*	とう

NUMBERS OF CHINESE ORIGIN

1	**ichi** *(ee-chee)*	いち
2	**ni** *(nee)*	に
3	**san** *(sahn)*	さん
4	**shi/yon** *(she/yoan)*	し／よん
5	**go** *(go)*	ご
6	**roku** *(roe-koo)*	ろく
7	**shichi/nana** *(she-chee/nah-nah)*	しち／なな
8	**hachi** *(hah-chee)*	はち
9	**kyū/ku** *(koo/cue)*	きゅう／く
10	**jū** *(joo)*	じゅう

After ten only the Chinese numbers are used. Eleven is a combination of ten plus one **jū-ichi** *(joo-ee-chee)* じゅう いち, twelve is ten plus two **jū-ni** *(joo-nee)* じゅうに, and so on. Twenty is two tens **ni-jū** *(nee-joo)* にじゅう, thirty is three tens **san-jū** *(shan-joo)* さんじゅう, and so on.

11	**jū-ichi** *(joo-ee-chee)*	じゅういち
12	**jū-ni** *(joo-nee)*	じゅうに
13	**jū-san** *(joo-shan)*	じゅうさん
14	**jū-yon** *(joo-yoan)*	じゅうよん
	jū-shi *(joo-she)*	じゅうし
15	**jū-go** *(joo-go)*	じゅうご
16	**jū-roku** *(joo-roe-koo)*	じゅうろく
17	**jū-nana** *(joo-nah-nah)*	じゅうなな
	jū-shichi *(joo-she-chee)*	じゅうしち
18	**jū-hachi** *(joo-hah-chee)*	じゅうはち
19	**jū-kyū** *(joo-cue)*	じゅうきゅう
	jū-ku *(joo-koo)*	じゅうく
20	**ni-jū** *(nee-joo)*	にじゅう
21	**ni-jū-ichi** *(nee-joo-ee-chee)*	にじゅういち
22	**ni-jū-ni** *(nee-joo-nee)*	にじゅうに
23	**ni-jū-san** *(nee-joo-sahn)*	にじゅうさん
24	**ni-jū-yon** *(nee-joo-yoan)*	にじゅうよん
	ni-jū-shi *(nee-joo-she)*	にじゅうし
25	**ni-jū-go** *(nee-joo-go)*	にじゅうご
30	**san-jū** *(sahn-joo)*	さんじゅう
31	**san-jū-ichi** *(sahn-joo-ee-chee)*	さんじゅういち
32	**san-jū-ni** *(sahn-joo-nee)*	さんじゅうに
40	**yon-jū** *(yoan-joo)*	よんじゅう
50	**go-jū** *(go-joo)*	ごじゅう
60	**roku-jū** *(roe-koo-joo)*	ろくじゅう
70	**shichi-jū** *(she-chee-joo)*	しちじゅう
	nana-jū *(nah-nah-joo)*	ななじゅう
80	**hachi-jū** *(hah-chee-joo)*	はちじゅう
90	**kyū-jū** *(cue-joo)*	きゅうじゅう

100	**hyaku** (*h'yah-koo*)	ひゃく
101	**hyaku-ichi** (*h'yah-koo-ee-chee*)	ひゃくいち
102	**hyaku-ni** (*h'yah-koo-nee*)	ひゃくに
120	**hyaku ni-jū** (*h'yah-koo nee-joo*)	ひゃくにじゅう
121	**hyaku-ni-jū-ichi**	ひゃくにじゅういち
	(*h'yah-koo nee-joo-ee-chee*)	
130	**hyaku-san-jū**	ひゃくさんじゅう
	(*h'yah-koo sahn-joo*)	
140	**hyaku-yon-jū**	ひゃくよんじゅう
	(*h'yah-koo yoan-joo*)	
200	**ni-hyaku** (*nee h'yah-koo*)	にひゃく
300	**san-byaku** (*sahn b'yah-koo*)	さんびゃく
500	**go-hyaku** (*go h'yah-koo*)	ごひゃく
600	**roppyaku** (*rope-p'yah-koo*)	ろっぴゃく
800	**happyaku** (*hape-p'yah-koo*)	はっぴゃく
1,000	**sen** (*sen*)	せん
	issen (*ee-ssen*)	いっせん
1,100	**sen-hyaku**	せんひゃく
	(*sen-h'yah-koo*)	
1,200	**sen-ni-hyaku**	せんにひゃく
	(*sen-nee-h'yah-koo*)	
2,000	**ni-sen** (*nee-sen*)	にせん
3,000	**san-zen** (*sahn-zen*)	さんぜん
5,000	**go-sen** (*go-sen*)	ごせん
8,000	**hassen** (*hah-ssen*)	はっせん
10,000	**ichi-man** (*ee-chee-mahn*)	いちまん
11,000	**ichi-man-issen**	いちまんいっせん
	(*ee-chee-mahn-ee-ssen*)	
20,000	**ni-man** (*nee-mahn*)	にまん
50,000	**go-man** (*go-mahn*)	ごまん
100,000	**jū-man** (*joo-mahn*)	じゅうまん
200,000	**ni-jū-man** (*nee-joo-mahn*)	にじゅうまん
500,000	**go-jū-man** (*go-joo-mahn*)	ごじゅうまん
1,000,000	**hyaku-man**	ひゃくまん
	(*h'yah-koo-mahn*)	

75 hitori *(shh-toe-ree)*
one person ひとり

76 futari *(fu-tah-ree)*
two persons ふたり

When referring to one or two persons, the native Japanese counting system is used.

➡ (We are) two persons. ふたり　です。
Futari desu. *(fu-tah-ree dess)*

The Chinese number system is used when counting people from three on up. When you enter a restaurant, the host will use **nan mei sama desu ka**? *(nahn may sah-mah dess kah)* なんめいさま　です　か。 to ask, "How many persons are there?" In this instance **nan** means "how many" instead of "what," **mei** is another way of saying "person," and **-sama** is an honorific form of **san**. If you are a party of two you can answer **futari desu** or **ni mei desu**.

77 san-nin *(sahn neen)*
three persons さんにん

➡ (We are) three persons. さんにん　です。
Sannin desu. *(sahn neen dess)*

78 yo-nin *(yo-neen)*
four persons よにん

➡ (We are) four persons. よにん　です。
Yonin desu. *(yo-neen dess)*

79 **jikan** *(jee-kahn)*
time, hour じかん

ichi-jikan *(ee-chee jee-kahn)*
one hour いちじかん

ni-jikan *(nee jee-kahn)*
two hours にじかん

san-jikan *(sahn jee-kahn)*
three hours さんじかん

yo-jikan *(yo jee-kahn)*
four hours よじかん

go-jikan *(go jee-kahn)*
five hours, etc. ごじかん

nan-jikan? *(nahn jee-kahn)*
how many hours? なんじかん？

Time is expressed the following way:

ichi-ji *(ee-chee jee)*	one o'clock	いちじ
ni-ji *(nee jee)*	two o'clock	にじ
san-ji *(sahn jee)*	three o'clock	さんじ
yo-ji *(yo jee)*	four o'clock	よじ
go- ji *(go jee)*	five o'clock	ごじ
roku-ji *(roe koo jee)*	six o'clock	ろくじ
shichi-ji *(shee-chee jee)*	seven o'clock	しちじ
hachi-ji *(hah-chee jee)*	eight o'clock	はちじ
ku-ji *(koo jee)*	nine o'clock	くじ
jū-ji *(joo jee)*	ten o'clock	じゅうじ

jū-ichi-ji	eleven o'clock	じゅういちじ
(joo ee-chee jee)		
jū-ni-ji *(joo nee jee)*	twelve o'clock	じゅうにじ
nan-ji? *(nahn jee)*	what time?	なんじ？

80 fun/pun *(hoon/poon)*
minute, minutes ふん／ぷん

ippun *(eep-poon)*	one minute	いっぷん
ni-fun *(nee-hoon)*	two minute	にふん
san-pun *(sahn-poon)*	three minute	さんぷん
yon-pun *(yoan-poon)*	four minute	よんぷん
go-fun *(go-hoon)*	five minutes	ごふん
roppun *(rope-poon)*	six minutes	ろっぷん
nana-fun	seven minutes	ななふん
(nah-nah-hoon)		
happun *(hahp-poon)*	eight minutes	はっぷん
kyū-fun *(cue-hoon)*	nine minutes	きゅうふん
juppun *(joo-poon)*	ten minutes	じゅっぷん
jū-ippun	eleven minutes	じゅういっぷん
(joo-eep-poon)		
jū-ni-fun	twelve minutes	じゅうにふん
(joo-nee-hoon)		
ni-juppun	twenty minutes	にじゅっぷん
(nee-joop-poon)		
san-juppun	thirty minutes	さんじゅっぷん
(sahn-joop-poon)		
yon-jū-go-fun	forty-five minutes	よんじゅうごふん
(yoan-joo-go-hoon)		
nan-pun?	how many minutes?	なんぷん？
(nan-poon)		

Japanese Dialects

Students of the Japanese language and especially short-term visitors who attempt to learn just enough to get by, generally do not have to worry about Japanese dialects because virtually all Japanese understand **hyōjungo** (*h'yoe-june-go*) ひょうじゅんご which is the standard language spoken in Tokyo.

However, even beginning students of the language will immediately pick up on differences in the accents and vocabulary of residents of Tokyo, Kyoto, Osaka, Købe, and other cities. Dialects that are basically unintelligible to students of standard Japanese include those spoken in Kagoshima on the southern end of Kyushu island and Aomori in northeastern Honshu (the main island).

There are dozens of other regional dialects different enough that the speakers are instantly recognizable as natives of certain areas. Some of these dialects are so different from standard Japanese that people who are not from those areas often do not understand what is being said.

PART 9
Words 81–90

81 gozen (*go-zen*)
morning (AM) ごぜん

82 gogo (*go-go*)
afternoon (PM) ごご

➡ It is ten-thirty in the morning.
　ごぜん　じゅうじ　さんじゅっぷん　です。
　Gozen jū-ji san-juppun desu.
　(*go-zen juu-jee sahn-joop-poon dess*)

➡ I shall meet (you) this afternoon at two o'clock.
　きょう　の　ごご　にじ　に　あいます。
　Kyō no gogo ni-ji ni aimasu.
　(*k'yoe no go-go nee-jee nee aye-mahss*)

➡ Let's go this afternoon.
　きょう　の　ごご　に　いきましょう。
　Kyō no gogo ni ikimashō.
　(*k'yoe no go-go nee ee-kee-mah-show*)

➡ Let's go tomorrow afternoon.
　あした　の　ごご　に　いきましょう。
　Ashita no gogo ni ikimashō.
　(*ahssh-tah no go-go nee ee-kee-mah-show*)

Han (*hahn*) はん, meaning "half" is also used to express
the half hour, as in **ni-ji han** (*nee-jee hahn*) にじはん or
2:30.

83 takushii *(tahk-she)*
taxi タクシー

- ➡ I want to go by taxi. タクシー で いきたい です。
  Takushî de ikitai desu. *(tahk-she day ee-kee-tai dess)*

- ➡ Please call a taxi. タクシー を よんで ください。
  Takushî o yonde kudasai.
  (tahk-she oh yoan-day koo-dah-sai)

- ➡ Let's go by taxi. タクシー で いきましょう。
  Takushî de ikimashō. *(tahk-she day ee-kee-mah-show)*

84 chikatetsu *(chee-kah-tet-sue)*
subway, metro, underground ちかてつ

- ➡ Where is the subway? ちかてつ は どこ です か。
  Chikatetsu wa doko desu ka?
  (chee-kah-tet-sue wah doe-koe dess kah)

- ➡ I want to go by subway. ちかてつ で いきたい です。
  Chikatetsu de ikitai desu.
  (chee-kah-tet-sue day ee-kee-tai dess)

- ➡ Shall we go by subway? ちかてつ で いきましょう か。
  Chikatetsu de ikimashō ka?
  (chee-kah-tet-sue day ee-kee-mah-show kah)

- ➡ Let's go by subway. ちかてつ で いきましょう。
  Chikatetsu de ikimashō.
  (chee-kah-tet-sue day ee-kee-mah-show)

85 densha *(den-shah)*
train でんしゃ

➡ Shall we go by train? でんしゃ で いきましょう か。
Densha de ikimashō ka?
(den-shah day ee-kee-mah-show kah)

➡ Let's go by train. でんしゃ で いきましょう。
Densha de ikimashō. *(den-shah day ee-kee-mah-show)*

➡ Is it better to go by train?
でんしゃ で いく ほう が いい です か。
Densha de iku hō ga ii desu ka?
(den-shah day ee-koo hoh gah ee dess kah)

86 eki *(eh-kee)*
station えき

➡ Where is the station? えき は どこ です か。
Eki wa doko desu ka? *(eh-kee wah doe-koe dess kah)*

87 chikai *(chee-kai)*
near ちかい

➡ Where is the nearest subway station?
いちばん ちかい ちかてつ は どこ です か。
Ichiban chikai chikatetsu wa doko desu ka?
(ee-chee-bahn chee-kai chee-kah-tet-sue wah doe-koe dess kah)

➡ How much is it by subway from here to the Ginza?
ここ から ぎんざ まで ちかてつ で いくら で
す か。
Koko kara Ginza made chikatetsu de ikura desu ka?
(koe-koe kah-rah geen-zah mah-day chee-kah-tet-sue day ee-koo-rah dess kah)

Kara *(kah-rah)* から means "from."

88 shinkansen *(sheen-kahn-sen)*
Bullet Train しんかんせん

Shinkansen literally means "New Trunk Line," but it is
almost always translated into English as "Bullet Train" or
"Bullet Trains". Some of these famous trains, launched in
1964, cruise at over 321.869 kph (200 miles per hour).

➡ I want to go by Bullet Train.
しんかんせん　で　いきたい　です。
Shinkansen de ikitai desu.
(sheen-kahn-sen day ee-kee-tai dess)

➡ Does the Bullet Train stop in Shin Yokohama?
しんかんせん　は　しん　よこはま　に　とまりますか。
Shinkansen wa Shin Yokohama ni tomarimasu ka?
*(sheen-kahn-sen wah sheen Yokohama nee toe-mah-ree-
mahss kah)*

➡ Yes, it does stop (there). とまります。
Tomarimasu. *(toe-mah-ree-mahss)*

Actually, some do and some don't, depending on which
category.

89 atsui *(aht-sue-ee)*
hot (weather and to the touch) あつい

➡ It is really hot today!
きょう　は　ほんとう　に　あつい　です。
Kyō wa hontō ni atsui desu.
(k'yoe wah hone-toe nee aht-sue-ee dess)

Hontō *(hone-toe)* ほんとう means "real" and **hontō ni**
(hone-toe nee) ほんとう　に means "really."

➡ It's hot today, isn't it! きょう は あつい です ね。
   Kyō wa atsui desu ne! *(k'yoe wah aht-sue-ee dess nay)*

   Ne *(nay)* ね, when it occurs at the end of a sentence, is equivalent to an English "question tag," such as "... isn't it!" or "... don't they!" etc.

➡ Is the sake hot? さけ が あつい です か。
   Sake ga atsui desu ka? *(sake gah aht-sue-ee dess kah)*

90 samui *(sah-moo-ee)*
   cold (weather), to feel cold さむい

➡ It's cold, isn't it! さむい です ね。
   Samui desu ne! *(sah-moo-ee dess nay)*

➡ Are you cold? さむい です か。
   Samui desu ka? *(sah-moo-ee dess kah)*

➡ No, I'm not cold. いいえ、さむくない です。
   Iie, samukunai desu. *(eee-eh, sah-moo-koo nai dess)*

Giving Up on Japanese!

Prior to the dissolution of the Tokugawa shogunate in 1868, Japan was divided into more than 200 fiefs presided over by hereditary lords called **Daimyō** *(daimeyoe)* だいみょう, literally "Great Names." Many of these fiefs functioned more or less as autonomous districts, with their own unique dialects. Travel was tightly controlled and there was no national mass media to bind the people or languages together.

The diversity of dialects and the difficulty encountered in learning how to write the complicated Chinese characters (adopted between the 4th and 6th centuries A.D.) was such an enormous problem that some of the leaders of the early Meiji period (which followed the Tokugawa shogunate system of government) suggested that the nation give up Japanese and adopt English as the official language of the country. Needless to say, this was not a very popular suggestion.

Now, Japanese is widely taught around the world, and many foreigners have become fluent in the language.

PART 10
Words 91–100

91 **tsumetai** *(t'sue-may-tai)*
cold (to the touch) つめたい

→ This water is cold! この みず は つめたい です。
Kono mizu wa tsumetai desu.
(koe-no mee-zoo wah t'sue-may-tai dess)

92 **kōhii** *(koe-hee)*
coffee コーヒー

→ Hot coffee, please. ホット コーヒー を ください。
Hotto kōhī o kudasai. *(hot-toe koe-hee oh koo-dah-sai)*

→ Iced coffee, please. アイス コーヒー を ください。
Aisu kōhī o kudasai. *(eye-sue koe-hee oh koo-dah-sai)*

93 **miruku** *(me-rue-koo)*
milk ミルク

→ Cold milk, please. つめたい ミルク を ください。
Tsumetai miruku o kudasai.
(t'sue-may-tai me-rue-koo oh koo-dah-sai)

94 **ame** *(ah-may)*
→ rain あめ

95 **yuki** *(yoo-kee)*
snow ゆき

96 furimasu *(fuu-ree-mahss)*
to fall, come down　ふります

- ➡ It is raining.　あめ　が　ふって　います。
  Ame ga futte imasu. *(ah-may gah fuut-tay ee-mahss)*

- ➡ It is snowing.　ゆき　が　ふって　います。
  Yuki ga futte imasu. *(yoo-kee gah fuut-tay ee-mahss)*

- ➡ Will it rain tomorrow?　あした　あめ　が　ふります　か。
  Ashita ame ga furimasu ka?
  (ahssh-tah ah-may gah fuu-ree-mahss kah)

- ➡ No, it will not rain.　いいえ、ふりません。
  Iie, furimasen. *(ee-eh, fuu-ree-mah-sen)*

97 byōki *(b'yoe-kee)*
sick　びょうき

98 isha *(ee-shah)*
doctor　いしゃ

- ➡ I'm sick, please call a doctor.
  びょうき　です。いしゃ　を　よんで　ください。
  Byōki desu. Isha o yonde kudasai.
  (b'yoe-kee dess, ee-shah oh yoan-day koo-dah-sai)

99 aruku *(ah-rue-koo)*
to walk　あるく

  Arukimasu. *(ah-rue-kee-mahss)*
  I shall walk.　あるきます。

Arukimasen. *(ah-rue-kee-mah-sen)*
I shall not walk. あるきません。

Arukimasu ka? *(ah-rue-kee-mahssh kah)*
Do we walk? Shall we walk? あるきますか。

Arukitai desu. *(ah-rue-kee-tai dess)*
I want to walk. あるきたい　です。

Arukimashō ka? *(ah-rue-kee-mah-show kah)*
Shall we walk? あるきましょう　か。

Arukimashō. *(ah-rue-kee-mah-show)*
Let's walk. あるきましょう。

Arukimashita. *(ah-rue-kee-mahssh-tah)*
I walked. あるきました。

Arukemasen *(ah-rue-kay-mah-sen)*
I cannot walk. あるけません。

100 tōi *(toy)*
far, distant とおい

➡ Is it (very) far? とおい　です　か。
Tōi desu ka? *(toy dess kah)*

➡ Is it possible to walk from here?
ここ　から　あるけます　か。
Koko kara arukemasu ka?
(koe-koe kah-rah ah-rue-kay-mahss kah)

➡ Yes, it is not far. はい、とおくない　です
Hai, tōkunai desu. *(hi, toe-koo nai dess)*

➡ No, it is (too) far. いいえ、とおい　です。
Iie, tōi desu. *(eee-eh, toy dess)*

Special Set Phrases

There are a number of set expressions in Japanese that are an important part of the country's formal etiquette system. These terms are used daily and contribute significantly to the flavor of the culture. Using them adds a very polite and natural nuance to your speech.

Irasshaimase! *(ee-rah-shy-mah-say)*
Welcome ! いらっしゃいませ。

Tadaima! *(tah-dai-mah)*
I'm home! (I've returned!) ただいま。

O-kaeri nasai! *(oh-kai-eh-ree nah-sai)*
Welcome back (home)! おかえり　なさい。

O-jama shimasu. *(oh-jah-mah she-mahss)*
I am intruding. Excuse me. おじゃま　します。

This is a polite term used when you enter someone's home, office, or private room.

O-jama shimashita. *(oh-jah-mah she-mahssh-tah)*
I have intruded. I have bothered you. Goodbye.
おじゃま　しました。
This is said when you leave a home or office you have been visiting.

Shitsurei shimasu. *(sheet-sue-ray she-mahss)*
Excuse me. I'm sorry. しつれい　します。

This term is used when you pass in front of someone (as in a theater or while walking through a crowd). It is also used when entering or leaving someone's office, and when hanging up the phone.

Shitsurei shimashita. *(sheet-sue-ray she-mahssh-tah)*
Sorry for disturbing (bothering) you.
しつれい　しました。

This is said when you interfere with some person or situation (as when you bump into someone, mistakenly walk into an office or meeting room that is being used, or cause any kind of minor disturbance).

Itadakimasu. *(ee-tah-dah-kee-mahss)*
I receive, accept (the food, drink). いただきます。

Mentioned earlier in the **100 Key Word Section** as "I shall receive (something)," this term is used regularly just before beginning to eat or drink, especially when someone else is the host, and also by family members in their own home. It is a courteous expression of thanks and appreciation and, although it is not religious in nature, it has the same ritualistic feel as the saying of grace before a meal.

O-somatsu sama. *(oh-so-maht-sue sah-mah)*
It was nothing. おそまつさま。

When you have a meal at a private home and thank the cook, this is the term he or she is most likely to use in response. Its figurative meaning is "It was nothing, but thank you for mentioning it."

O-kagesama de. *(oh-kah-gay sah-mah day)*
Thanks to you. Thank you for asking.
おかげさま　で。

This is often said as a response when someone asks you how you are, or how a friend or family member is doing, or how things are going. In essence it means "Thank you for asking..." and is followed by "I'm doing fine," "He or she is fine," etc.

Gokurōsama deshita.
(goe-koo-roe-sah-mah desh-tah)
Thanks for all your hard work. Well done.
ごくろうさま　でした。

This ceremonial expression literally means something like "It has been a situation of honorable bitter toil." It is commonly used as a way of expressing thanks to someone who worked hard and is finished for the day. Like the English "Well done," it should not be used to people one has to be especially polite to.

O-negai shimasu. *(oh-nay-guy she-mahss)*
O-negai itashimasu *(oh-nay-guy ee-tah-she-mahss)*
Please (do something for the speaker). I beg of you. おねがい　します。/おねがい　いたします。

These polite terms are used, virtually interchangeably, when asking a favor from someone or some kind of special consideration or help. They are complete sentences in themselves and are generally used after the speaker has asked the other party to do something or accept some obligation.

Yoroshiku o-negai shimasu.
(yoe-roe-she-koo oh-nay-guy she-mahss)

Yoroshiku o-negai itashimasu.
(yoe-roe-she-koo oh-nay-guy ee-tah-she-mahss)
Please (do something for the speaker) (very polite). よろしく　おねがい　します。/よろしく　おねがい　いたします。

Both **o-negai shimasu** and **o-negai itashimasu** are commonly preceded by **yoroshiku** *(yoe-roe-she-koo)* よろしく and a bow, which significantly increases the power of the request and turns it into a serious appeal.

Common Everyday Expressions

O-genki desu ka? *(oh-gen-kee dess kah)*
How are you? Are you well? おげんき　です　か。

Genki desu. (person's name)-san wa?
(gen-kee dess, …sahn wah)
I'm fine. And you? げんき　です。…さん　は。

O-tenki wa ii desu, ne!
(oh-ten-kee wah eee dess nay)
The weather is fine, isn't it!
おてんき　は　いい　です　ね。

Shō-shō o-machi kudasai.
(show-show oh-mah-chee koo-dah-sai)
Just a moment, please. (polite)
しょうしょう　おまち　ください。

Chotto matte! *(choat-toe maht-tay)*
Just a second! Hang on! (informal)
ちょっと　まって。

Dō itashimashite. *(doe-ee-tah-she-mahssh-tay)*
Don't mention it. You're welcome.
どう　いたしまして。

Hajimemashite. *(hah-jee-may-mahhssh-tay)*
Pleased to meet you. はじめまして。

Additional Vocabulary

A

address	**jūsho** *(juu-show)*	じゅうしょ
age	**toshi** *(toe-she)*	とし
air-conditioning		
	eakon *(ayj-ah kone)*	エアコン
airmail	**kōkūbin** *(koe-koo-bean)*	こうくうびん
airplane	**hikōki** *(he-koe-kee)*	ひこうき
airport	**kūkō** *(koo-koe)*	くうこう
April	**shigatsu** *(she-got-sue)*	しがつ
arrive	**tsukimasu**	つきます
	(t'sue-kee-mahss)	
August	**hachigatsu**	はちがつ
	(hah-chee-got-sue)	
automobile	**jidōsha** *(jee-doe-shah)*	じどうしゃ

B

bank	**ginkō** *(geen-koe)*	ぎんこう
bar	**bā** *(bah)*	バー
bath	**o-furo** *(oh-fuu-roe)*	おふろ
beautiful	**utsukushii**	うつくしい
	(oo-t'sue-koo-shee)	
beef	**bīfu** *(bee-fuu)*	ビーフ
birthday	**tanjōbi** *(tahn-joe-bee)*	たんじょうび
book	**hon** *(hone)*	ほん
bookstore	**hon'ya** *(hone-yah)*	ほんや

box lunch (Japanese-style)

	o-bentō *(oh-ben-toe)*	おべんとう
bread	**pan** *(pahn)*	パン
breakfast	**asagohan** *(ah-sah-go-hahn)*	あさごはん
bridge	**hashi** *(hah-she)*	はし
building	**biru** *(be-rue)*	ビル
bus	**basu** *(bah-sue)*	バス

C

cabaret	**kyabarē** *(k'yah-bah-ray)*	キャバレー
camera	**kamera** *(kah-may-rah)*	カメラ
car	**kuruma** *(koo-rue-mah)*	くるま
chair	**isu** *(ee-sue)*	いす

change (money returned)

| | **o-tsuri** *(oh-t'sue-ree)* | おつり |

change (small coins)

	kozeni *(koe-zay-nee)*	こぜに
children	**kodomo** *(koe-doe-moe)*	こども
chopsticks	**o-hashi** *(oh-hah-she)*	おはし
cold (illness)	**kaze** *(kah-zay)*	かぜ
catch a cold	**kaze o hikimasu**	かぜ を ひきます
	(kah-zay oh he-kee-mahss)	

congratulations

	omedetō gozaimasu	おめでとうございます
	(oh-may-day-toe go-zai-mahss)	
corner	**kado** *(kah-doe)*	かど
cover charge	**kabā chāji**	カバー チャージ
	(kah-bah- chah-jee)	

D

date (time of the month)

	hizuke *(he-zoo-kay)*	ひづけ
daughter	**musume** *(moo-sue-may)*	むすめ
daytime	**hiruma** *(he-rue-mah)*	ひるま

day after tomorrow

| | **asatte** *(ah-saht-tay)* | あさって |

December	**jū-ni-gatsu**	じゅうにがつ
	(juu-nee-got-sue)	
deliver	**todokemasu**	とどけます
	(toe-doe-kay-mahss)	
dentist	**ha-isha** *(hai-shah)*	はいしゃ
departure	**shuppatsu** *(shupe-pot-sue)*	しゅっぱつ
deposit (for room)		
	tetsukekin	てつけきん
	(tay-tsue-kay-keen)	
dessert	**dezāto** *(day-zah-toe)*	デザート
dining car	**shokudōsha**	しょくどうしゃ
	(show-koo-doe shah)	
dining room	**shokudō** *(show-koo-doe)*	しょくどう
dinner, evening meal		
	yūshoku	ゆうしょく
	(yuu-show-koo)	
drink	**nomimono**	のみもの
	(no-me-moe-no)	
discount	**waribiki**	わりびき
	(wah-ree-bee-kee)	
dollar	**doru** *(doe-rue)*	ドル
double room	**daburu rūmu**	ダブル　ルーム
	(dah-boo-rue rue-moo)	
driver	**untenshu** *(oon-ten-shoo)*	うんてんしゅ
drugstore	**yakkyoku** *(yahk-k'yoe-koo)*	やっきょく
drycleaning	**dorai kuriiningu**	ドライクリーニング
	(doe-rye koo-ree-neen-goo)	

E

east	**higashi** *(he-gah-she)*	ひがし
eel	**unagi** *(oo-nah-ghee)*	うなぎ
embassy	**taishikan** *(tai-she-kahn)*	たいしかん
egg	**tamago** *(tah-mah-go)*	たまご
England	**Igirisu** *(ee-ghee-ree-sue)*	イギリス
entrance	**iriguchi** *(ee-ree-goo-chee)*	いりぐち

evening	**yūgata** *(yuu-gah-tah)*	ゆうがた
this evening	**konban** *(kome-bahn)*	こんばん
exit	**deguchi** *(day-goo-chee)*	でぐち
express train	**kyūkō** *(cue-koe)*	きゅうこう
expressway, motorway		
	kōsokudōro	こうそくどうろ
	(koe-soe-koo-doe-roe)	
eye	**me** *(may)*	め
glasses, spectacles		
	megane *(may-gah-nay)*	めがね

F

fall, autumn	**aki** *(ah-kee)*	あき
February	**ni-gatsu** *(nee-got-sue)*	にがつ
fee	**tesūryō** *(tay-sue-r'yoe)*	てすうりょう
festival	**o-matsuri**	おまつり
	(oh-maht-sue-ree)	
fever	**netsu** *(neh-t'sue)*	ねつ
first-class (tickets)		
	fāsuto kurasu	ファーストクラス
fish	**sakana** *(sah-kah-nah)*	さかな
foreign	**gaikoku no**	がいこく　の
	(guy-koe-koo)	
foreigner	**gaikokujin**	がいこくじん
	(guy-koe-koo-jeen)	
France	**Furansu** *(fuu-rahn-sue)*	フランス
front desk, reception desk		
	furonto *(fuu-roan-toe)*	フロント
fruit	**kudamono**	くだもの
	(koo-dah-moe-no)	

G

gallery	**gyararî** *(g'yah-rah-ree)*	ギャラリー
garden	**niwa** *(nee-wah)*	にわ
garlic	**ninniku** *(neen-nee-koo)*	にんにく

genuine	**honmono no**	ほんもの　の
	(home-moe-no no)	
Germany	**Doitsu** *(doe-ee-t'sue)*	ドイツ
get off (disembark)		
	orimasu *(oh-ree-mahss)*	おります
I get on, embark		
	norimasu *(no-ree-mahss)*	のります
glasses (spectacles)		
	megane *(may-gah-nay)*	めがね
gram	**guramu** *(goo-rah-moo)*	グラム
guest	**o-kyakusan**	おきゃくさん
	(oh-k'yah-koo sahn)	

H

hand	**te** *(tay)*	て
hanger (for clothing)		
	hangā *(hahn-gah)*	ハンガー
heart attacks	**shinzō mahi**	しんぞう　まひ
	(sheen-zoe mah-hee)	
heavy	**omoi** *(owe-moy)*	おもい
holiday	**kyūjitsu** *(cue-jee-t'sue)*	きゅうじつ
home	**uchi** *(oo-chee)*	うち
horseradish	**wasabi** *(wah-sah-bee)*	わさび
hospital	**byōin** *(b'yoe-een)*	びょういん
hot (spicy)	**karai** *(kah-rye)*	からい
hot spring	*onsen* *(own-sen)*	おんせん
house (structure)		
	ie *(ee-eh)*	いえ
hungry	**onaka ga sukimasu**	おなか　が　すきます
	(oh-nah-kah gah ski-mass)	
hurry	**isogimasu**	いそぎます
	(ee-so-ghee-mass)	
painful, sore	**itai** *(ee-tai)*	いたい

I

inn (Japanese style)

ryokan *(r'yoe-kahn)* りょかん

international **kokusai** *(coke-sai)* こくさい

international telephone (call)

kokusai denwa こくさいでんわ
(koke-sai den-wah)

intersection, crossroads

kōsaten *(koe-sah-ten)* こうさてん

introduce **shōkai shimasu** しょうかいします

introduction (written)

shōkaijō *(show-kai-joe)* しょうかいじょう

J

January **ichi-gatsu** いちがつ
(ee-chee-got-sue)

Japan **Nihon** *(nee-hone)* にほん

Japanese-style bed

futon *(fuu-tone)* ふとん

Japanese-style room

nihon-ma にほんま
(nee-hone-mah)

job **shigoto** *(she-go-toe)* しごと

July **shichi-gatsu** しちがつ
(she-chee-got-sue)

June **roku-gatsu** ろくがつ
(roe-koo-got-sue)

K

key **kagi** *(kah-ghee)* かぎ

kilogram **kiro** *(kee-roe)* キロ

kilometer **kiro** *(kee-roe)* キロ

kind (nice) **shinsetsu** *(shin-set-sue)* しんせつ

English	Japanese (romaji)	Japanese (kana)
Korea (South)	**Kankoku** *(kahn-koe-koo)*	かんこく
Korean (language)		
	Kankokugo *(kahn-koe-koo-go)*	かんこくご
Korean (person)		
	Kankoku-jin *(kahn-koe-koo-jeen)*	かんこくじん

L

last (final)	**saigo** *(sai-go)*	さいご
last day	**saigo no hi** *(sai-go no hee)*	さいご の ひ
last month	**sengetsu** *(sen-get-sue)*	せんげつ
last week	**senshū** *(sen-shoo)*	せんしゅう
last year	**kyonen** *(k'yoe-nen)*	きょねん
laundry	**sentakumono** *(sen-tah-koo-moe-no)*	せんたくもの
left (direction/side)		
	hidari *(he-dah-ree)*	ひだり
letter	**tegami** *(teh-gah-me)*	てがみ
luggage	**nimotsu** *(nee-moat-sue)*	にもつ
lunch	**hirugohan** *(he-rue-go-hahn)*	ひるごはん

M

maid	**meido** *(may-e-doe)*	メイド
man (male)	**otoko** *(oh-toe-koe)*	おとこ
manager	**manējā** *(mah-nay-jah)*	マネージャー
map	**chizu** *(chee-zoo)*	ちず
March	**san-gatsu** *(sahn-got-sue)*	さんがつ
May	**go-gatsu** *(go-got-sue)*	ごがつ
meal ticket	**shokken** *(shoke-ken)*	しょっけん
meat	**niku** *(nee-koo)*	にく
medicine	**kusuri** *(koo-sue-ree)*	くすり
menu	**menyū** *(men-yuu)*	メニュー
morning	**asa** *(ah-sah)*	あさ
movie	**eiga** *(a-e-gah)*	えいが

N

name card	**mēshi** *(may-she)*	めいし
napkin	**napukin** *(nahp-keen)*	ナプキン
New Year's	**o-shō-gatsu** *(oh-show-got-sue)*	おしょうがつ
next	**tsugi** *(t'sue-ghee)*	つぎ
next month	**raigetsu** *(rye-get-sue)*	らいげつ
next week	**raishū** *(rye-shoo)*	らいしゅう
next year	**rainen** *(rye-nane)*	らいねん
night	**yoru** *(yoe-rue)*	よる
nightclub	**naito kurabu** *(nai-toe koo-rah-boo)*	ナイト　クラブ
north	**kita** *(kee-tah)*	きた
November	**jū-ichi-gatsu** *(juu-ee-chee-got-sue)*	じゅういちがつ

O

October	**jū-gatsu** *(juu-got-sue)*	じゅうがつ
once	**ichido** *(ee-chee-doe)*	いちど
one-way (street)	**ippō tsūkō** *(eep-poe t'sue-koe)*	いっぽうつうこう
one-way (ticket)	**kata-michi** *(kah-tah-mee-chee)*	かたみち
onions	**tamanegi** *(tah-mah-nay-ghee)*	たまねぎ

P

package, parcel	**kozutsumi** *(koe-zoot-sue-me)*	こづつみ
paper	**kami** *(kah-me)*	かみ
park, recreational area	**kōen** *(koe-en)*	こうえん

parking	**chūshajō**	ちゅうしゃじょう
	(choo-shah-joe)	
passport	**pasupōto**	パスポート
	(pah-sue-poe-toe)	
pearls	**shinju** *(sheen-juu)*	しんじゅ
pepper	**koshō** *(koe-show)*	こしょう
platform (train)	**hōmu** *(hoe-moo)*	ホーム
police box (small sub-station on street)		
	kōban *(koe-bahn)*	こうばん
policeman	**o-mawari-san**	おまわりさん
	(oh-mah-wah-ree-sahn)	
porter	**pōtā** *(poe-tah)*	ポーター
post office	**yūbinkyoku**	ゆうびんきょく
	(yuu-bean k'yoe-koo)	
potatoes	**jagaimo**	じゃがいも
	(jah-guy-ee-moe)	
pottery	**tōki** *(toe-kee)*	とうき
public telephone		
	kōshū denwa	こうしゅうでんわ
	(koe-shoo den-wah)	

R

refrigerator	**reizōko** *(ray-e-zoe-koe)*	れいぞうこ
refund	**harai-modoshi**	はらいもどし
	(hah-rye-moe-doe-she)	
rent	**yachin** *(yah-cheen)*	やちん
repair	**naoshimasu**	なおします
	(nah-oh-she-mahss)	
reservation	**yoyaku** *(yoe-yah-koo)*	よやく
reserved seat	**shiteiseki** *(ssh-tay-seh-kee)*	していせき
restaurant (Japanese)		
	ryōriya *(rio-ree-yah)*	りょうりや
restaurant (Western)		
	resutoran *(res-toe-ran)*	レストラン

rice (cooked white rice)		
	gohan *(go-hahn)*	ごはん
right (direction/side)		
	migi *(mee-ghee)*	みぎ
road	**michi** *(mee-chee)*	みち
room	**heya** *(hay-yah)*	へや
room (Japanese-style)		
	nihon-ma *(nee-hone-mah)*	にほんま
room (Western-style)		
	yō-ma *(yoe-mah)*	ようま
room number	**rūmu nambā** *(rue-moo nahm-bah)*	ルーム　ナンバー
room service	**rūmu sābisu** *(rue-moo sah-bee-sue)*	ルーム　サービス

S

salt	**shio** *(she-oh)*	しお
schedule (plan)	**yotei** *(yoe-tay)*	よてい
school	**gakkō** *(gahk-koe)*	がっこう
sea (ocean)	**umi** *(oo-me)*	うみ
seamail	**funabin** *(fuu-nah-bean)*	ふなびん
seasick	**funayoi** *(fuu-nah-yoe-e)*	ふなよい
seaside	**kaigan** *(kai-gahn)*	かいがん
season	**kisetsu** *(kee-set-sue)*	きせつ
seat	**seki** *(seh-kee)*	せき
seat number	**zaseki bangō** *(zah-say-kee)*	ざせき　ばんごう
September	**ku-gatsu** *(koo-got-sue)*	くがつ
service center	**sābisu sentā** *(sah-bee-sue sen-tah)*	サービス　センター
ship	**fune** *(fuu-nay)*	ふね
shirt	**shatsu** *(shah-t'sue)*	シャツ
shrine	**jinja** *(jeen-jah)*	じんじゃ
single room	**shinguru** *(sheen-goo-rue)*	シングル

slow	**yukkuri** *(yuke-koo-ree)*	ゆっくり
soap	**sekken** *(sek-ken)*	せっけん
son	**musuko** *(moo-sue-koe)*	むすこ
south	**minami** *(me-nah-me)*	みなみ
souvenir (gift)	**omiyage** *(oh-me-yah-gay)*	おみやげ
soy sauce	**shōyu** *(show-yoo)*	しょうゆ
spicy	**karai** *(kah-rye)*	からい
spoon	**supūn** *(su-poon)*	スプーン
spring	**haru** *(hah-rue)*	はる
stamp (for mail)		
	kitte *(keet-tay)*	きって
stop (bus/train)	**teiryūjo** *(tay-e-r'yoo-joe)*	ていりゅうじょ
straight (direction)		
	massugu	まっすぐ
	(mahss-sue-goo)	
sugar	**satō** *(sah-toe)*	さとう
summer	**natsu** *(not-sue)*	なつ
supermarket	**sūpā** *(sue-pah)*	スーパー

T

table	**tēburu** *(tay-boo-rue)*	テーブル
tag (label)	**harigami**	はりがみ
	(hah-ree-gah-me)	
taxi stand	**takushî noriba**	タクシー　のりば
	(tock-she no-ree-bah)	
tea (black/brown)		
	kōcha *(koe-chah)*	こうちゃ
tea (Japanese green tea)		
	nihon-cha	にほんちゃ
	(nee-hone-chah)	
television	**terebi** *(tay-ray-bee)*	テレビ
temperature (body)		
	taion *(tai-own)*	たいおん
temperature (weather)		
	ondo *(own-doe)*	おんど

temple	**o-tera** *(oh-tay-rah)*	おてら
theater (movies)		
	eigakan *(a-e-gah-kahn)*	えいがかん
ticket	**kippu** *(keep-poo)*	きっぷ
ticket window (vending machines)		
	kippu uriba *(keep-poo oo-ree-bah)*	きっぷ　うりば
toilet	**o-tearai** *(oh-tay-ah-rye)*	おてあらい
tonight	**konban** *(kome-bahn)*	こんばん
traffic	**kōtsū** *(kote-sue)*	こうつう
traffic light	**shingō** *(sheen-go)*	しんごう
traveler's checks		
	toraberāzu chekku *(toe-rah-bay-rah-zoo check-ku)*	トラベラーズ　チェック
twin room (two persons, two beds)		
	tsuin *(t'sue-ween)*	ツイン

V

vegetables	**yasai** *(yah-sai)*	やさい
visa	**biza** *(bee-zah)*	ビザ

W

waiter	**uētā** *(way-tah)*	ウエーター
washroom	**o-tearai** *(oh-tay-ah-rye)*	おてあらい
way (direction)	**iku michi** *(ee-koo me-chee)*	いく　みち
weather	**tenki** *(ten-kee)*	てんき
weather forecast		
	tenki yohō *(tane-kee yoe-hoe)*	てんきよほう
west	**nishi** *(nee-she)*	にし
window	**mado** *(mah-doe)*	まど

winter	**fuyu** (*fuu-yoo*)	ふゆ
women	**onna no hito**	おんな　の　ひと
	(*own-nah no ssh-toe*)	
wonderful	**subarashii**	すばらしい
	(*sue-bah-rah-she*)	

Y

yesterday	**kinō** (*kee-no*)	きのう
young	**wakai** (*wah-kai*)	わかい
youth hostel	**yūsu hosuteru**	ユースホステル
	(*yoo-sue hos-tay-rue*)	

Z

| zoo | **dōbutsuen** | どうぶつえん |
| | (*doe-boot-sue-en*) | |